The Team Builder's Textbook

Building Communities in the Information Age

D0967894

CHRIS BRADY AND ORRIN WOODWARD

The
Team
Builder's
Textbook

Building Communities in the
Information Age

Second Edition, January 2007

Published by:

Obstacles Press, Inc.
PO Box 1109
Grand Blanc, MI 48439

Cover design and layout by Norm Williams
Comic illustrations by Sean Catron

Printed in the United States of America

"Our greatest fear should not be of failure, but of succeeding at something that doesn't really matter.
- D. L. Moody

Dedication

This book is dedicated to you, the Team business owner. May
you experience all the success you are prepared to earn!

Acknowledgements

We would like to say thank you to our wives, Terri Brady and Laurie Woodward, for unyielding love, support, understanding, and flexibility. We would also like to thank our parents, Jim and Gayle Brady and Orrin "Bud" and Kathy Woodward for their examples and encouragement.

Thanks are also due to Bob Dickie III, and the entire staff at Obstacles Press, Inc., and to our very talented cartoonist, Sean Catron. Graphic artwork and book assembly was artfully performed by Norm Williams.

And as always and in everything, we give all the honor and glory to our Lord and Savior Jesus Christ. Everything we have and will ever accomplish is by His grace.

Table of Contents

Introduction

The Internet Age is upon us; there is no arguing it. The Industrial Age is over and the Information Age is here. The old world and the old ways are gone. The diagram below gives a brief oversight of how new ages displace old ones, and how this process is happening faster than it ever has before.

AGRARIAN AGE   INDUSTRIAL AGE   INFORMATION AGE

The world-renowned economist Paul Zane Pilzer, in *The Next Millionaires*, said, "The Internet represents one of the greatest economic revolutions in history – and it's just getting started. The impact of the Internet, which is even now only in its infancy, can only be compared to the invention of writing, which created the birth of civilization, and the printing press, which created industrialization." Statistics are certainly readily available to support Pilzer's claims. There are more people online than ever before. There are more people *shopping* online than ever before. And the amount the average electronic commerce shopper is spending continually goes up.

Michael Dell, billionaire founder of Dell Computers, gave a speech to the Detroit Economic Club in November of 1999. In that talk he outlined the importance of being in business and capitalizing on the enormous trends of the Internet. Dell stipulated that to be in business and not be involved in the explosiveness of the Information Age would be to miss the greatest business opportunity of our lifetime. Further, Dell explained the concept of developing "communities" of loyal, enthusiastic customers *online*. Anybody can build a website, and nearly everyone has. Anybody can invest some money and fill a warehouse with products to sell through that website, and many companies have. But it takes something *more* to develop a base of customers, or in Dell's words, a "community" of shoppers that will return to the website again and again. Conventional advertising techniques have proven largely ineffective. More contemporary approaches such as banner adds and referral kickbacks have also performed poorly. For these reasons, despite an exploding customer base, most companies have actually *failed* at developing significant web traffic for their products!

Something more is needed, something that will build and sustain enthusiasm and loyalty on the part of the customer, something that will bring them back repeatedly and cause them to bring their friends. That "something" is called *business ownership,* or a "piece of the action." With the enormous cost reductions possible through the Internet, such as elimination of the retail store, advertising, and several distribution steps, there is ample revenue that can be shared among a body of owners to reward them for developing a customer base. Such a plan brings the idea of Internet business down to the level of the individual. In a nutshell, that is the *opportunity* side of the business; a chance to build communities of people who share a financial interest in developing electronic commerce. That opportunity has proven to work well. It requires very little money to initiate, operate, or expand. It involves no complicated licensing or qualification procedures. Quitting one's current means of employment is unnecessary, and bank loans or building mortgages are not required. The upside is unlimited, while the entrance requirements are extremely low. And it is an opportunity available to anyone with basic ambition and an eagerness to learn.

Having a great *opportunity* is the **first component** of wealth. One simply cannot create wealth where no opportunity exists. Why is it that the most inventions and patents, the most research papers, and the most technological advancements come out of free countries? Why is there almost a ratio that shows that the freer the country the more prolific the opportunities? And why is it that those same countries are the wealthiest? The reason is because opportunity must be available before wealth can be created.

Former Ohio Congressman Bob McEwen states, "The greater the freedom, the greater the wealth."

The **second component** of wealth is *proper thinking*. Opportunity is one thing. Taking advantage of it is another. It takes knowledge, wisdom, and experience to build and sustain wealth. As an example, consider a lottery. When an individual wins a state-sponsored lottery, generally there is a large sum of money at stake. Without any special abilities, character development, or specialized knowledge and experience, an individual has suddenly received enormous financial means. Certainly, at least for the winning individual, the lottery proves to be a great opportunity. But without the proper thinking, without experience and wisdom, wealth is nearly always fleeting. Many, many lottery winners not only squander their winnings, but usually end up filing for bankruptcy! This means that the new onrush of funds came in and hijacked the old, pre-existing funds! As this demonstrates, opportunity itself, even if enormous, is not able by itself to create wealth; for wealth to be created, experience and knowledge must accompany opportunity.

Getting involved with the Team provides one with the very unique chance to have *both* opportunity *and* wealth-thinking. This book is about this second component. No matter how great the business opportunity is (and it is great), one must know how to utilize it, build it, and sustain it for its full potential to be realized. Building communities of people associated with online commerce is not a common skill. If it were, large retailers and manufacturers would already be doing it successfully. They have certainly tried! But community building is a special expertise, one in which the Team and its leaders have proven adept by leading their field for years. Tens of thousands of business owners throughout the western hemisphere plug into the Team's training system on a regular basis to learn the expertise of building communities. Audio recordings, books, pamphlets, messaging systems, seminars, and national conventions comprise a training strategy with proven, systematic results. It is structured and presented from two very important levels:

1. Principles
2. Specifics (methods)

To build a community of people through which electronic commerce takes place, and to establish a profitable business, *both* principles *and* specifics must be learned. The old axiom is, "Methods are many, principles are few, methods always change, but principles never do." The Team training system comprises *both* aspects of education by embodying principles that are timeless and methods that are timely. This book is similarly structured. The reader will not only uncover the principles required to build and sustain a profitable community, but will become familiar with specific techniques that work in the field today. This book, *The Team Builder's Textbook,* organizes the key concepts and areas of expertise that the Team has developed over the years into a highly readable, yet easily accessible format. It comprises the overall framework of building a community and makes liberal references to additional training aids that can provide deeper understanding of particular concepts or techniques.

The story is told of a young man who graduated from high school and took a job in a sporting goods store. One day a wealthy customer entered and purchased a large sum of items with cash. The young man decided to assist the customer as he transported his goods out to the parking lot. Along the way the curious young man posed the question, "How do I get to be successful like you, someday?" The customer stopped and looked the young man over for a moment, never before having been asked a question that wise. After considering his reply, the customer said, "First, determine what you want in life. Second, find someone who has accomplished it and learn all you can from them. Third, go do what they did." With that, the customer got into his car and drove off. The young man never even got the man's name, but he did get a piece of advice that made him wealthy. While most of us know what we want in life, it becomes very difficult to find someone who has success and is interested in teaching us how they accomplished it. This book takes care of that step. It shows and teaches a clearly marked path to success and significance, one that involves *Having*

Fun, Making Money, and Making a Difference in people's lives, all while exploiting the enormous potential of the Internet, the Information Age, and the New Economy. All that is left for the reader to do is apply it.

Chapter 1

Dreams
The Power of "Why"

Carl Sandburg said, "Nothing happens without first a dream." If we don't know what we're shooting for, we'll probably never hit it. Or said another way, if we aim at nothing we will hit it with amazing accuracy.

The first step in building a strong and profitable business is to understand why you're doing it in the first place. It seems so elementary that many people will say, "I know what I want, teach me how to get it!" or "You teach me how to make the money and I'll know how to spend it." But success doesn't work that way. Knowing *why* is much more important than knowing *how.* Don't get us wrong; this book is all about teaching the *how.* But success can never be obtained without a strong enough *why.* The reason for this is that the *why* provides the energy and motivation required to execute the *how.* "Not me," some say, "I'm self-motivated!" Wrong again. Normally the person that makes a statement like that has very little success in life. They haven't needed motivation because they haven't accomplished anything! Rest assured; true success will require a strong *why.*

Dreams

The professional background of each of the authors was engineering. Nowhere, ever, were we taught to make use of the word "dream." There was no Dream 101 course. There was no way to calculate the strength of a Dream. There was no need to even know the word in order to build parts for cars. Besides, any engineer worth his salt knows that such talk is hokey. Engineers (and probably most professions) don't talk about dreams. Instead, they talk about goals, objectives, strategies, action items, deliverables, standards, and other exciting corporate buzzwords. But never the

1

word "dream."

We are quite certain most people share a similar opinion about dreams. But this book isn't about *most people*, it's about people who want to excel and succeed, it's about people who want to live incredible lives; it's about people who choose to rise above the lure of mediocrity and strive for excellence. Because of that, it is important to consider not what *most people* do with the concept of dreams, but what *extraordinary people* think about dreams.

Author and speaker Norman Vincent Peale said, "To achieve anything significant, everyone needs a little imagination and a big dream." Former President of the United States Woodrow Wilson said, "All big men are dreamers. They see things in the soft haze of a spring day or in the red fire of a long winter's evening. Some of us let our dreams die, but others nourish and protect them, nurse them through bad days till they bring them to sunshine and light, which always come to those who sincerely believe that their dreams will come true." Somehow, when said like that, the idea of dreams doesn't sound so hokey anymore!

Nearly everything we see and experience in the world that comes from the efforts of our fellow man is the result of what once began as only a dream. The paper you are holding in your hands, the light by which you read, the furniture upon which you sit were all first conceived in the mind of a dreamer before they were brought to reality. That's the power of dreaming. It changes the world for the better.

One man who had a dream was William Lloyd Garrison. Born during the early 1800's, Garrison dreamed of what must have seemed an impossible dream: abolishing slavery. According to author Walt Kallestad, "Garrison dared to dream this in a day when slavery in the United States, in the North as well as the South, was economically profitable and firmly entrenched. The influential governing body of one church declared that slavery was instituted by God. Key national figures insisted that the whole nation depended on slavery." But Garrison had a dream. For over thirty years he risked his life and fortune to publish an abolitionist newspaper called *The Liberator.* Among others, such as Frederick Douglass, Sojourner Truth, and Harriet Beecher Stowe,

Garrison's voice for the abolition of slavery eventually turned the tide of popular opinion, and an impossible dream came true.

Walt Disney dreamed of creating a permanent carnival where children could play and their parents could be free of worry. The park would be safe, the sidewalks impeccably clean, and the fun creatively crafted to entertain people of all ages. He risked the entire fortune he'd amassed by drawing cartoon characters, and went heavily into debt to see his dream launched. Disney not only created the world's most attended attractions, he invented an entirely new form of entertainment: the modern day theme park.

Dreams aren't fantasies or wishes. They aren't something for which someone hopes. Dreams are deep burning desires that drive the dreamer to create and accomplish and perform. W. Clement Stone said, "When you discover your mission, you will feel its demand. It will fill you with enthusiasm and a burning desire to get to work on it." That's the power of a dream; it grips you and won't let go. It drives you to step outside your comfort zone and reach for greatness. Dreams are special because they are sign posts to our destiny.

Getting a *Why*

There are many levels of dreams. There are dreams that are material or "surface level." There are others that are deeper and more meaningful. Still others transcend success and enter the realm of significance. Further still are the dreams that are concerned with personal destiny, God's purpose in our lives, and leaving a legacy. Whether a dream is big or small, or shallow or deep, it is the effect it has on the dreamer that is important. To begin correctly, one must clearly identify a dream or multiple dreams that provide food for the soul. A dream grasps the attention of a person and won't let go. It dominates his thoughts and fuels his ambition. To neglect the power of dreams and their impact on our performance is to leave unused one of life's biggest levers.

To help you identify in as clear a fashion as possible those dreams that will motivate and drive you to perform, grab a pen and answer the following questions. Take your time. Have some fun. Dream a little! This step is easy, fun, and free. Even so, don't underestimate it. Don't rush past this section looking for the "specifics." To paraphrase Henry Ford, an expert on *how* always works for an expert on *why*. So start with *why!*

1. What would you do if you knew you couldn't fail? (In other words, what would you do if you were guaranteed to succeed?)
2. What would your life be like in five years if you could design it yourself? Answer this question in terms of several categories:
   a. family life
   b. fitness and health
   c. financial
   d. career/profession
   e. friendships
   f. faith life.
3. What did you enjoy doing as a child that you always wished you would have pursued as an adult?
4. How do you want to be remembered? Write your own epitaph as it would be if you died today. Now rewrite it as though you accomplished all your dreams.

There are hundreds of questions that could be used to help clarify one's dreams, but keeping the list to these four allows the reader a chance to deeply contemplate each one.

There is a haunting folk song written and performed by *The Crash Test Dummies* with the lyrics,

> *I'm still young,*
> *but I know my days are numbered;*
> *one, two, three, four, five, six, seven and so on.*
> *But the time will come*
> *when these numbers have all ended,*
> *and all I've ever seen will be forgotten.*

Our days are numbered. They are finite. It is important that we remember this. More so, not one of us knows the *number* of our days. It follows that we should therefore treat each day as a special gift from God. Sadly, though, we have each squandered time as though it had no value. We have each lived days and weeks and months and perhaps even years as if we were going to live forever. Almost two millennium ago the Roman Emperor Marcus Aurelius, said "Do not live as though you have a thousand years."

Renowned college football coach Lou Holtz in his book *Winning Every Day* tells the story of a student football player on his Notre Dame team named Alton Maiden. On a trip to Ireland, Maiden and the rest of the team made a sight seeing trip to a twelfth-century monastery. While walking through the tiny graveyard nearby, Maiden was inspired to write a poem called *The Dash*, which concludes as follows:

After death has come and gone, a tombstone sits for many to see.
But it serves no more than a symbol of a person's memory.
Under the person's name it reads the date of birth – and the date the person passed.
But the more I think about the tombstone the only important thing is the dash.
Yes, I see the name of the person but that I might forget.
I also read the date of birth and death, but even that might not stick.
But thinking about the person, I can't help but to remember the dash
Because it represents a person's life and that will always last.
So when you begin to chart your life, make sure you are on a positive path
Because people may forget your birth and death, but they will never forget your dash.
(emphasis added).

We are all in our *dash* right now. What we do matters. What we do leaves a memory. As the Gray Wizard in the movie *The Lord of the Rings* said, "The only question is, what will you do with the time you've been given?" Your real dream is the answer to that question.

The business is very flexible. Its rewards can be molded to fit the accomplishment of just about any dream someone may have. No matter how big or powerful someone's dream, success with the Team business can provide money and time and a network of relationships toward the fulfillment of that dream. As powerful as the business opportunity is, and as effective as the Team leadership training system is, none of it works unless the business owner has a clearly defined dream.

Dreams Aren't Fantasies

It is important at this point to warn the reader of something. Over our years in business, we have seen hundreds of people who could fill out a list of "the things they want." They can wax poetic about big houses, fancy cars, fabulous vacations, fine wardrobes, and time with family. They talk about buying an aircraft or racing cars. They speak of African safaris and trips to the moon. But when it comes to doing the work to earn these wonderful things, they sit on the couch and make excuses. These people are not dreamers, they are fantasizers. This is *not* what we mean by dreaming. Making a fanciful list of all the wonderful things in which one is interested has a very small motivational effect. It is little more than materialism.

What we mean by dreaming is finding something that speaks to your inner core, something that whispers deeply to who you really are inside, something that resonates with the deepest fiber of your being. A real dream packs a wallop. It grabs a hold of you and won't let go. It is on your mind day and night. A real dream is something that you just *have* to accomplish. A real dream is something you are *supposed* to achieve. A dream or vision is tomorrow's reality expressed as an idea today.

Dreams Aren't Free

Dreams are precious. Dreams are powerful. But dreams aren't free. A real dream requires a price to be paid for its fulfillment. Once one works to clearly define his or her dream, it is important to understand that commitment will be required to accomplish it. There will be no "something for nothing" when pursuing a true, God-Given dream. As the saying goes, success is always on the other side of inconvenience.

These truths all apply to the Team business, as well. There will be work involved. There will be commitments required. We will need to learn and do new things. For the fulfillment of a dream, we will be required to expand the boundaries of our comfort zone.

Finally, it is important to understand that our commitment and work are not for the *business,* but for our *dreams.* The business is just a vehicle that takes one to his or her dreams. We don't buy a car because we want to drive a car. We buy it because, first and foremost, we want it to take us somewhere. A secondary consideration is how much fun we have or how stylish we look or how fast we go getting there. So it is with the Team business; it is designed to get us to the accomplishment of our dreams, and along the way we will certainly learn to enjoy the ride, but the key is that it gets us to our dreams. It requires effort, and it is so worth it!

Personal Stories

Names: Tim & Amy Marks
Former Occupations: Engineer and Real Estate Divestor-Sales; Cosmetic Sales

I said, "Hey, I want to do that!" It was Easter Sunday (a key point) somewhere in the early 1980s and we were at my grand parent's to celebrate the holiday. Two of my uncles had just come from work and still had on their work clothes. To a young industrious boy, this looked way cool. As the afternoon went on, I sat watching my uncles and wondered if they would tell any cool stories from work. They didn't. They did, however, ask me a question that would set the course for my life (at least until I met Bill). The profound question they asked me was, "Timmy, what are you going to do when you grow up?" Well, I sat there looking at them and thought about how they had made all this money on Easter Sunday, and I knew they got to wear work boots and coveralls and such. What else would I say? "I am going to work in the shop!"

So I did. I started out welding, then went on to become an electrician (don't tell anyone). One day, I was working in a foundry running some conduit when I noticed some guys drinking coffee and watching me work. I asked my Journeyman, "What the *#$%@ do those guys do?"

"They are engineers," he said. Well, that was all I needed! If I could drink coffee and watch people work, I would go to any amount of college they wanted me to. So I went to college three nights a week, and studied on the off-nights, in order to remember all the things I would never use and would soon forget. The company I was working for at the time noticed I liked my job so much that they gave me all kinds of responsibilities and **authority** (not good for a choleric). I soon found myself spending more time "in the shop" than I did at home, which was justified because I was doing it "for the family." Right. It only took about nine years of 60 to 90 hours a week, and Amy almost leaving me, for me to wake up to the fact that I was married, but *not* to my job.

8

The next great idea I had, which was designed to fix all this, was to get involved in real estate investing, specifically: rental homes. The only problem was that I was a bit short on start-up capital. So I borrowed a few grand from my 401k and we were off! Well, *I* was. Amy hated this as much as my job. I told her, "Honey, this is it!" I really believed that I would have *time and money*, even though nobody I ever met in the rental business did. But who cares, right? Don't get all hung up on the FACTS! This escapade lasted for about two years. I started to realize that it was not going to make me rich or happy.

Have you ever looked back at some of the milestones in you life and thought, "Wow, I didn't even know that was a milestone?" Such as the "Easter Sunday advice" or the "I want to be an engineer" thought I had without doing any research? Well, I now realize that one of the biggest milestones in my life was when Bill got Amy and me to an Open Meeting and we saw our future, or rather, our destiny.

Sometimes Amy and I say, "We wish we could have seen the plan sooner," or, "Man, we could have avoided a lot of heartache and headaches." But you know what? God has a perfect plan for us, and I'm glad He put us through those things, because now we can appreciate the many blessings we have. And they're all through God's grace and all that the Team has done for us!

Names: Mark and Jenn Paul
Former Occupations: Engineer and Executive of Strategic Sales for Distribution Business; Hospitality Manager, Fitness Instructor and Real Estate Agent

When Jenn and I first met, we would meet every week on Thursday nights at the same restaurant and dream about what we would do if we won the lottery. We would spend hours talking about having a house in Hawaii; starting the day by surfing in the morning and getting back to the house and eating a fresh pineapple for breakfast. In the afternoon, we talked of riding Harley's to the gym. In the evenings, it would be making dinner and curling up together to watch a movie. If that became old, we could fly to a condo in Colorado and ski in the winter, mountain bike and hike in the summer. The only problem was that we hadn't won the lottery, and we both had jobs that we didn't like in Michigan.

It was December 31, 1999, New Years eve - the end of the millennium and the beginning of the next. We made a decision that night to leave it all behind and begin living our dreams. I went into work on the first day of the new millennium and put in my two week notice. The dream began! We moved to Telluride, Colorado and lived among the rich and famous, skiing by day, and hitting the spa in the evening to work out and relax in the saunas. The only problem was the money that we had was quickly fading away. I received a call from a friend back in Michigan who was interested in selling his manufacturing business that he had operated for about 15 years. We left our dream behind to buy a job. A lawsuit ended that business and we found ourselves asking, what do we do now? How do we spend time together, live our dreams, and create an income?

Somehow, our reasoning led us into real estate. At least we could work together, and I figured that if I had to, I could always go back into the automotive industry and earn a six figure income. But I knew that there had to be more. The first week in real estate, Jenn and I were riding around with the broker to learn the ropes. The first stop was a house that we had to measure so that we could meet with the owner later in the day to hopefully get the listing. The odd thing was that whoever had lived in the house had left a lot behind; old furniture, bedding and towels. The next stop was going to be at a friend of the broker's who was selling him a house on land contract. When we pulled up to the friend's residence, the broker warned us that he was involved in some "internet business". We knocked on the door and were introduced to Tim Marks. I had known Tim's older brother from high school. When the land contract was signed, the broker went into the other room to make a copy of the paperwork. I asked Tim what he did for a living. (What I was trying to ask politely was "How are you home during the day and live in a house like this, and you are younger than me?") He asked if I had ever heard of Orrin Woodward. I said, yes! I had gone to college with Orrin. Tim asked if I also knew Chris Brady. Yes! Orrin and Chris had both gone to GMI Engineering and Management Institute (now Kettering University) and they had worked at the same GM location that I had. Tim asked if I knew of their accomplishments and I told him that I hadn't seen either since college. Tim then told me that he had gotten into business with them and that he would be willing to sit down with me the following evening to discuss what they were doing. I said, "sure!"

When we left Tim's house, the broker was shocked that I had known Orrin and Chris. He said that the house that we had measured earlier that day was Orrin's old house and that the reason that possessions were left behind was that when he bought his new mansion, that he had purchased *everything* new! I certainly didn't know any of my friends that had done something like that, especially any engineers. The broker then told us that we would be stopping at Orrin's new home next to see if we could get the listing on the house that we had measured earlier. We pulled up in front of a huge home. I was thinking to myself, "There is no way this is the guy that I went to college with." Deep inside I was thinking, "Please don't let this be the same guy," because that would mean that he had made it and that I hadn't. I rang the door bell and Orrin opened the door and said, "Well hello, Mark! How have you been?" All of a sudden I wasn't feeling so good. I told Orrin that I had just met Tim Marks and that we were going to sit down the next evening to discuss what they were doing. Orrin edified Tim, telling me what an excellent business partner Tim was and that he would totally be able to explain what they were doing.

When I left Orrin's house, I couldn't wait for the next evening to hear what Orrin, Chris and Tim had their hands on. The next evening finally came and Jenn and I went over to Tim and Amy Marks' house. I didn't really care what they were doing. **I just wanted the results that I had seen the day before.** They had been home during the day with their families, had nice homes, and seemed happy and stress free. Tim drew out the business plan, and all I remember was Tim asking Jenn and me what would we do if time and money were unlimited. It brought me back to those Thursday nights that Jenn and I would sit at that restaurant and dream about life. I saw a business that could get those very results. I thought that if these guys that I had known from college thought that this was a good idea, and they had achieved the results that I could see, I was in! This was our chance to achieve everything that we had ever imagined. This was the vehicle that could get us that morning surf in Hawaii, and those long, snow-covered runs in Colorado. We had won the lottery, only better! We just had to do the work. We knew that we wouldn't have to do this alone. We would have a mentor and a proven system. We could do this! And so the journey began...

"Until you give yourself to some great cause, you haven't begun
to fully live."
- John Mason

"Every man dies, not every man really lives."
- Mel Gibson as William Wallace in the movie *Braveheart*

"Never let your fears stand in the way of your dreams."
- unknown

"Why not go out on a limb? Isn't that where the fruit is?"
- Frank Sculley

"It isn't where you come from, it's where you're going that
counts."
- Ella Fitzgerald

Name: SANDY SPORTS

Quote: "Sounds great! I'll be ready to get going as soon as my softball league finishes up. Oh, and my Tuesday night bowling league. Did I mention that I play beach volleyball every other weekend?"

Chapter 2

Wealth-Thinking
How You Think Determines How You Live

How we think is the most critical element in our success. How we see the world, how we interpret what we see, and what we decide based upon those interpretations is called *thinking*. As philosopher Francis Shaeffer explained, all our thoughts are skewed by something called our *world view*. This is basically the lens through which we see and interpret all that is around us. To be successful financially requires proper wealth-thinking, and this can only happen from a correct perspective or world view.

As the ancient Greek philosopher Epictetus wrote in *Discourses*, "Appearances to the mind are of four kinds. Things either are what they appear to be; or they neither are, nor appear to be; or they are and do not appear to be; or they are not, and yet appear to be. Rightly to aim in all these cases is the wise man's mark." Just trying to figure out what Epictetus is talking about is more thinking than most of us want to do! Maybe that's why Henry Ford said, "Thinking is the hardest work there is, that's why so few people engage in it." Hard work or not, thinking is *the* element in success.

Someone once asked, "Why do some people make it while others quit?" The answer lies in their differences in thinking. The Team business *will* work and *does* work, for anybody of any stripe. The reason *everybody* doesn't make it is because they fail in their thinking. Their non-successful actions then follow their wrong thinking. This is perhaps the most important principle we have to teach in this entire book. The secret is to get your thinking right. Once that is accomplished, success can follow.

There are thoughts that are enablers of success, and there are their opposites: *disablers* of success. One might call this second category "limiting beliefs." It would be quite easy to list a bunch of beliefs that we commonly come across when talking to people

15

about the Team business. But it is much more productive, we think (no pun intended), to consider a list of *enabling* thoughts, or "empowering beliefs," which are actually world view principles that will be required for success in any field, and certainly in building your team.

You Don't Know What You Don't Know

In order to develop proper thinking, it is important to have the attitude that we don't know everything already. If our finances are messed up, we don't have money figured out yet. If our relationships in life are messed up, we are not experts on dealing with people yet. The saying goes like this: *You don't know what you don't know.* We are the most ignorant about the things we are ignorant about. We don't even know that we don't know them. And this is precisely where we are hurt the most. Not knowing is what is holding us back.

Therefore, we had better become students. We had better prepare to learn, to love learning, and to learn for the rest of our lives.

What does this have to do with thinking, you might ask? Everything! Thinking you know it all is a sure sign that no success will be coming your way. Thinking that you have a lot yet to learn is a sure sign that you can succeed and achieve even beyond where you are in life already. Proper thinking begins with a proper perspective on learning and wisdom. Returning once again to ancient Greece, it was said that Socrates was the wisest man of all. When asked why this might be so, Socrates answered that if it were true, it was only because he was the only one in Athens who knew that he didn't know the answers. There must be something to it. We're talking about him thousands of years later!

Success Can Be Learned

Once we realize that we don't know it all, the next conclusion ought to be that we *can* learn it all! What!? You might say?

One of the most enabling, empowering ways of thinking is that if you don't know something, you could learn it if you wanted to badly enough. The fact that success can be learned is one of the most empowering beliefs a person can hold. While we certainly will never know it *all,* we can definitely learn what we need to succeed.

Tom Stoppard said, "Every ceiling, when reached, becomes a floor upon which one walks and now can see a new ceiling. Every exit is an entry somewhere." No matter where we are in life, we can move forward from where we are through learning. We like to use the analogy of water rushing along a ravine. It eddies and swirls violently and powerfully until it hits a dam, then it presses up against the dam and settles to a rest. Unless the dam is removed, the water goes no further. Our education (and we're not only referring to the *formal* kind here), is a lot like that rushing water. When we learn something new, it is a breakthrough in our lives. We rush forward to success. But then, if we come to the edge of our learning, we are halted in our progress until the next lesson is learned. Then we are freed up for another breakthrough and go tumbling toward more success.

That is what learning does; it allows us to flow in the direction of our dreams. But none of this would happen, however, if we didn't first have the empowering thought that we can learn what we need to succeed. Without that belief, without that proper thinking, we are dead in the water (so to speak).

You Are Worthy of Success

Knowing that we don't know it all and believing that we can succeed are not enough if we don't have a proper perspective about ourselves. It has been said that ninety-five percent of people have a low self-image, and the rest have a bad attitude. We don't know if that's true, but we have encountered scores of people who seem to think success is for "somebody else." This is destructive thinking of the highest order, and is just not true. Success is a door that is open to all. Walking through it is what is required. It will never be easy, it will never be "overnight," but it will be worth it, and anybody can become worthy of it.

"But you don't know about me," someone might say.

17

"You don't understand my circumstances," another might reply. "If you knew about my past, you'd never say I could still succeed."

"Success is not for people like me."

"I'm unlucky."

"I'm a victim."

We could continue this list for pages. But all of these replies (which we've actually heard many times) are lies. *You* can succeed. Yes, *you*. Everybody has had hard times. Everybody has had self-doubts. Everybody has regrets. Everybody has had bad breaks. But for every story of heartache, we can find someone, someplace who overcame much, much worse situations to achieve beyond most people's wildest dreams. It's all a matter of perspective. It's all a matter of *thinking*.

Believe you can and you can. Believe you can't and you can't. Either way, you are right. If you are prepared to learn what you need to learn, and do what you need to do, you can succeed. Period.

Dreamers Are in the Minority

Something else to understand when you decide to chase after success is that you will be in the minority. Everybody loves the *idea* of success, but few ever truly pursue it. When you decide to step out beyond the crowd, understand that the crowd does not like that. Proper thinking keeps this in perspective. Proper thinking dictates that to live in ways the common person cannot live will require doing things the common person will not do. Learn to become comfortable with being enthusiastic about something, even if those around you aren't.

Henry Wadsworth Longfellow said, "Not in the clamor of the crowded streets, not in the shouts or plaudits of the throng, but in ourselves are triumph and defeat." As author John Mason wrote, "More than anyone else, *you* must be persuaded." There is something singular about pursuing success. Comfort can be found in the crowd, but success is found in our individual dreams. Dreamers are a minority. Just like eagles, they are not found in flocks, they are found one at a time. Have the courage to stand on your own and stand for your dreams.

Criticism Is Normal for an Achiever

Courage will be required because criticism will accompany all great achievement. As Albert Einstein said, "Great spirits have always encountered violent opposition from mediocre minds."

This is a new concept for many people. It was for us, too. When we followed the common success strategy taught to us by well-meaning individuals who were steeped in the philosophy of the out-of-date Industrial Age (which was to go to school, get good grades, and get a good, secure job with benefits), we received nothing but praise. But following that advice got us into debt and committed almost all of our waking hours to working jobs that weren't getting us anywhere. All the while, we were applauded and congratulated on being so "successful." Then we became entrepreneurs and people lined up to tell us we were crazy. People who had never indicated any interest in our financial well-being before suddenly felt comfortable offering negative opinions about what we were doing! It seemed everybody had an opinion, and most of them were negative. Some were down-right critical.

Dale Carnegie said, "Any fool can criticize, condemn, and complain, and most do." The way to understand criticism is to realize that all great achievement meets with resistance. In fact, attracting a few good critics can be a key indicator that you are on the road to success!

Here is what we eventually came to learn: people are free to say and think whatever they want. But *they* weren't the ones responsible for our lives, families, or for paying our bills. It was up to us to decide what was best for our lives and to take the responsibility for our actions. That was one reason we worked and studied consistently to learn all we needed to learn to succeed. Not that we know everything now, we have a long way to go, but our learning and efforts did pay off. We were able to leave our jobs and live the lifestyles we had dreamt of. And we did it in spite of the critics. John Mason said, "There's always a heavy demand for fresh mediocrity – don't give in to it."

As famous nineteenth century author Edward Gibbon said, "I never make the mistake of arguing with people for whose opinions I have no respect." What we finally realized was that we should be seeking only the opinions of the people who had the results in life that we wanted to achieve ourselves. All other inputs were kindly ignored.

A Yiddish proverb says, "A critic is like the girl who can't dance so she says the band can't play." Don't worry about the criticism from those who can't dance. Focus instead on the music and don't miss your chance to dance!

Take the Long Term View

Another form of proper, wealth-thinking is to have a long term view of things. Too many people in our society today want instant food, instant cash, instant coffee, and instant success. What we have learned is that the more you demand *now*, the less you can have *later.*

In *The Cashflow Quadrant,* author Robert Kiyosaki wrote:

> There was a study done a number of years ago of rich and poor all around the world. The study wanted to find out how people born into poverty eventually become wealthy. The study found that these people . . . possessed three qualities. These qualities were:
>
> 1. They maintained a long term vision and plan
> 2. They believed in delayed gratification
> 3. They used the power of compounding in their favor
>
> The study found that these people thought and planned for the long term and knew that they could ultimately achieve financial success by holding to a dream or a vision. They were willing to make short term sacrifices to gain long-term success, the basis of delayed gratification.

Perhaps the best illustration of the importance of long term thinking is the power of compounding. Consider the often used demonstration of the penny doubling. Which appears to be more valuable: a million dollars paid in one lump sum; or a penny on the first day, added to double that amount on the second day, added to double that amount on the third day, and so on for just a month (we'll use thirty days)? Most of us have probably heard of this before, but it should never stop shocking us just how miraculously the penny doubling model adds up! Is it more than a million dollars? Way more! To be exact, it adds up to $10,737,418.23 (according to The Math Forum @ Drexel). No wonder Einstein famously quipped that compounding was the 8th Wonder of the World! If money compounds this fabulously given the power of time and accumulation; imagine what human energy can accomplish if applied to similar long term models of accumulation (such as the Team business)!

Notice the sub-point buried in all of this, too. How much money would you have on the first day? Just a penny. How much on the second day? Three cents. After five days you'd only have 31 cents! But yet five days is one sixth of the entire time allotted! On the fifteenth day, *half way into the allotted amount of time,* you'd have just $163.83! How many people get half-way into a worthy endeavor, only to give up because of "lack of results" or "not enough progress"? As this model shows, such people are severely misguided, and it stems from their lack of a long term view and their ignorance of the power of compounding.

There is another point here, as well. Sometimes, people will get the idea that those building this business are just in it for the money. To a certain extent, of course, that is true. This is a business, and one of the over-riding purposes of a business is to generate income for its owner(s). So money is entirely acceptable as an appropriate measure of a business's performance. But the very concept of the power of compounding means that there must be a period of time where things are allowed to compound; meaning that there is a requirement for delayed gratification, that period of time in which there is little or no money rolling in. During this period, there must be other allurements and blessings to capture the affections of the business owner, long before the money shows up. This is one of the reasons the Team has the motto: Have Fun, Make Money, and Make a Difference. In the early stages of business development, of course there is not going to be abundant wealth! Therefore, when one's first check is say, six dollars, he or she had better be having fun! And making a difference by serving and helping people can also happen immediately and along the entire journey, long before money shows up. Also, in our book *Launching a Leadership Revolution,* we introduced the concept of the Tri-Lateral Leadership Ledger; a concise way to measure one's personal, internal growth. As we build our businesses, we will become better in many areas of our lives. We will be learning the principles of success along with the specifics of the business. We will be improving our people skills. We will be learning goal setting and game planning skills. These and many other aspects of personal growth in the Team business journey are all blessings to be had that can and do come before the money does. All these things are important to keep in mind as one works to harvest the fruits of delayed gratification and the power of compounding.

Proper wealth-thinking always requires the long-term view of things. All good things take time. Delayed gratification and a mature expectation of the time required to obtain results are critical to accomplishing meaningful, lasting success. As President James Garfield said, "When God wants to grow a squash He grows it in one summer; but when He wants to grow an oak He takes a century."

Big Things Come From Little Things

One of the most successful athletic coaches of all time is Coach John Wooden. The summary of his achievements while head coach of the UCLA Bruins basketball team is staggering:

- 10 national championships (a record)
- Seven national championships in a row (a record)
- 88 consecutive victories (a record)
- 38 straight tournament playoff wins (a record)

- Four perfect seasons (a record)
- With only one losing year – his first – in 41 years of coaching!

His formula for success is both simple and surprising. One of his biggest precepts is the concept that "little things make big things happen." Wooden says, "Often we place such emphasis on distant goals that inadequate attention is given to what it takes to get there. To me, this is less about being a perfectionist and more about having a determination to be seeking improvement constantly. Success, not the devil, is in the details." Wooden maintains that there is a correct and most effective way to do everything. When coaching the UCLA Bruins, Wooden said, "I was not trying to create robots who simply did as they were told, but rather individuals who were *extremely* well grounded in the correct fundamentals, who had good performance habits. Little things, done well, make big things happen . . . ."

Understanding this simple but profound philosophy is crucial for building the Team business. This book is crammed full of details and fundamentals that, if mastered, can lead to enormous success. But to do that, they must be *mastered*. Doing enough of the right things in the right way for a long enough period of time is what produces success.

Take Responsibility

There is a famous saying which states, "If it's to be, it's up to me." While the Team business is distinguished for its ability to build teams of people, and its specialty of developing *communities* of people through which products and services flow, it might seem surprising to say "If it's to be, it's up to me." But that is exactly where success must start. In fact, most achievement is team or group achievement. Anything worthwhile in our lives involves other people. But the greatest explosion begins with a tiny spark. To build a team first requires the spark of an individual.

Taking personal responsibility for one's actions *and* the results of those actions is not an option for anyone desiring a successful life. British Prime minister, home secretary, first lord of the

Admiralty, chancellor of the exchequer, and perhaps the greatest Englishmen who ever lived, Winston Churchill said, "However tempting it might be to some, when much trouble lies ahead, to step aside adroitly and put someone else up to take the blows, I do not intend to take that cowardly course, but, on the contrary, to stand up to my post and persevere according to my duty . . . ." Churchill's example is one of proper thinking. Applied to the business owner's life, it will be an example of wealth-thinking also. The wealth in life finds its way into the hands of those who assume the most responsibility for their actions.

Focus Only Upon What You Can Control

Having a good attitude is another paramount principle of correct thinking. A good attitude results from a proper perspective on things. And a proper perspective leads us to work within our sphere of influence and leave the rest aside. The Bible says, "Sufficient unto the day is the evil thereof," (Matthew 6:34). Another way to say this is to focus only upon what you can control.

While we have just surveyed the importance of taking personal responsibility, we should guard against the tendency to assume responsibility for too much. What do we mean by too much? We mean things that are outside our area of influence. If something is beyond our ability to affect it, it should be beyond our ability to worry us. John Lubbock said, "A day of worry is more exhausting than a day of work." The most effective business owners are the ones who focus upon what they can directly control, and leave all the other things to the side. This keeps things simple and allows the business owner to focus on the steps he or she can take to bring about the desired future. Getting caught up in the little things or "under the circumstances" are destructive, distracting activities that lead to mediocrity. Focusing only upon what is important and under our immediate control is one of the golden strategies of wealth.

It's Not What Happens, It's How You Handle It

Another key aspect to having a good attitude is to realize that, as Stephen Covey says, "Between stimulus and response, we have a choice." We can choose how to respond. We like to say that "It's not what happens to you, it's how you respond that counts."

We will all have troubles and struggles. After all, problems are the price of success. The most successful people are the ones who respond maturely and appropriately to the challenges that come along. First, they analyze those problems in terms of the bigger picture. This brings a proper perspective as we discussed above. Next, they determine the most productive course of action instead of the natural, emotional one. Third, they take appropriate action with a good attitude. And finally, they monitor the results and learn from what results. This is all very easy to write about and to discuss in theory, but it is infinitely more difficult to put into practice in our lives. However, those that learn to think this way truly develop wealth-thinking and the positive results that go along with it.

Excuses are Useless, Except for Preventing Success

One thing you will never see is a champion who makes excuses. The two concepts simply cannot co-exist. According to Willis Whitney, "Some men have thousands of reasons why they cannot do what they want to do when all they really need is one reason why they can." And George Washington Carver said, "Ninety-Nine percent of failures come from people who have a habit of making excuses."

When a loser fails, he or she places blame or makes excuses. When a winner fails, he or she takes personal responsibility and admits his or her failings. In fact, it has been said that one is not a failure until he or she blames someone else or makes an excuse. Nursing pioneer Florence Nightingale said, "I attribute my success to this: I never gave or took an excuse." As the saying goes, "If you really want to do something, you'll find a way; if you don't, you'll find an excuse." Or perhaps it is better stated by saying, "If you don't want to do something, nobody can stop you!"

Commit to Your Dreams

The final aspect we'll consider in this section on wealth-thinking is commitment. Many people begin the journey of success in life, but few finish well. In fact, one commentator said there were four hundred leaders mentioned as influential in the Bible, but only about eighty of these "finished strong." Why is that? The answer is: a lack of commitment.

Author Joe Griffith said, "You cannot keep a committed person from success. Place stumbling blocks in his way, and he takes them for stepping-stones, and on them he will climb to greatness. Take away his money, and he makes spurs of his poverty to urge him on. The person who succeeds has a program; he fixes his course and adheres to it; he lays his plans and executes them; he goes straight to his goal. He is not pushed this side and that every time a difficulty is thrust in his way. If he can't go over it, he goes through it."

Any significant achievement will require a healthy dose of commitment. Football legend Vince Lombardi said, "There is only one way to succeed in anything and that is to give everything. I do and I demand that my players do. Any man's finest hour is when he has worked his heart out in a good cause and lies exhausted on the field of battle . . . victorious." That's commitment. And commitment produces another result, tenacity. As Lombardi also said, "The harder you work, the harder it is to surrender."

Personal Story

Names: Don and Chris Freeze
Former Occupations: International Consultancy, Business Owner; Divisional Comptroller of a Major Utility

Several years back, a friend asked me if I was looking for new consultants for my Value Engineering Consulting company. "Of course," was my response, "What can you tell me about the guy?" My friend described a young man named Orrin Woodward, a 29 year-old engineer who had four U.S. patents (several in production) and had just become the youngest winner of a prestigious national engineering award - the National Benchmarking award. Those credentials piqued my interest. I graduated from the same engineering undergrad school as this young man (GMI - General Motors Institute -- now Kettering University) and had been around engineers most of my adult life. Only a handful of them even had one patent to their name, let alone four. And the winner of a national engineering award is rare. I agreed to meet him for a coffee and size him up.

The first thing that impressed me about Orrin was his positive attitude. He was interested in checking out the world of consulting and he had done a smart thing. He asked a gentleman (my friend) who knew a lot of engineers and some engineering consultants to recommend some to him and vice-versa. I found out that Orrin was considering a career change, just as I had done when I left General Motors in 1987 to strike out on my own. He told me he had another business starting up, but was considering taking a short leave of absence from work, to do some consulting and make an informed life decision based on the experience. Smart. I asked him to develop a proposal for a Benchmarking study that I could deliver to some of the Vice Presidents of Engineering I knew from my years of consulting. If any of them expressed an interest, we could talk money. He agreed.

Orrin had an intensity about him that was compelling - which I realized was a passion for winning. You can see it in some men's eyes. I knew I was looking at a winner. But he wasn't cocky. He just had a calm confidence and an eagerness that I liked. And, Orrin was personable. I knew that when I got him in a conference room with an Engineering VP and a few of his staff that he could hold his own. I wasn't disappointed.

The client wanted the Benchmarking study. Orrin and I agreed to a $1,500 per diem. Of course I billed him out at my rate of $3,000 per day, so it was a true win-win arrangement. Things went well for about six weeks. Orrin called me to tell me he was finished working, and I assumed that he was referring to the project. I explained that the client was happy with the work and wanted additional studies. I also had other clients interested now that the tool had been proven. Orrin simply said, "No Don, I don't mean I'm finished with the project. What I mean is I'm finished working for you and General Motors. My other business is taking off." I was surprised to say the least.

After determining that he was serious, and that he hadn't won the lottery or inherited a large sum of money, I pointed out that at 31 years of age, he was too young to "retire". That's when he said, "Don, retirement has nothing to do with age. I'm not too young to retire; I'm making too much money to work." I was stunned. Nobody quits $1500/day and walks away from GM healthcare and retirement; especially with a non-working wife and four kids at home under the age of five. Nobody, that is, except Orrin Woodward, and a few people like him who know a better way. I had never met anyone who could pull off what Orrin was about to do. I asked him, "Well, what are you going to do all day?" He replied very simply, "I'm going to be a dad." That hit me like a ton of bricks. My kids had grown up while I was building my international consulting business. I stayed in touch by phone of course, but it's not the same as being there. You parents – and you young people – know exactly what I mean.

Anyway, I was intrigued. I wanted to know what he was doing. If it was really possible to make money and be home with your kids, I wanted to know about it. It was too late for me; my kids were finishing up high school and going off to college. But, if what Orrin was doing really worked, I could teach my kids the secret

28

and find some other folks who also really wanted to be full-time parents. Orrin said he'd help me and shared his Internet-based business plan with me.

I felt really tentative about trying this thing – I was the biggest skeptic you ever met, but I was looking for better results in life. Here was a guy who just walked away from $1,500 dollars a day, who was willing to show me what he was doing and I thought; what if this guy is the next Bill Gates or Michael Dell? He just might do something really big here! I'd better at least take a good hard look. I've heard Orrin Woodward quote so many leaders that I'm not sure which one of them said the following: "To be conscious that you are ignorant of the facts is a great step to knowledge." I am so glad that I did not let my ignorance and my ego keep me from this business. I almost did. But I remembered hearing someone else (I think it was my dad) say: "The greatest ignorance is to reject something you know nothing about." So I decided to do my due diligence. I researched it *all*. I ran a highly successful multinational engineering consulting company for 12 years. I had attorneys. When you do your due diligence, I'd highly recommend that you take advice ONLY from the people who have the kind of results in life that you want. Why would you do otherwise? Of course, be sure of what you want. And before you give anyone's opinion any credence at all, you should find out what kind of life they really have.

I just wanted to be debt free, not have to go to a job every day, have time and money to donate to church and charities and causes I believed in, have a healthy monthly passive income cash flow, spend more time with my wife and children and have great relationships with God, my family and my friends. Orrin Woodward had and has these results. That's why I decided to listen to him. He was the only person I had met in my 47 years on the planet that had all of it. He said he'd help and here's what I found out: If Orrin Woodward says something, you can take it to the bank!

So I signed on.

Orrin invited me to attend a seminar. I went to St. Louis and heard a presentation from a man named Robert Kiyosaki that completely changed my view of business and making money.

Then, one of my consulting partners, Greg, asked if I'd like to attend a business luncheon sponsored by the Detroit Economic Club of which he was a member. The speaker was to be Michael Dell. My thought process went like this: Dell has an Internet-Based business and I have an Internet-Based business. He was worth more than $21 Billion. I was not. Perhaps I might learn something. So I attended with Orrin Woodward, Chris Brady, my wife, and Greg. What Dell shared that day reinforced in every possible way what we were doing in this business!

Every successful person I have studied has applied these three steps to their lives: First, they clearly DEFINE what they want. Second, they find someone who has the results they want and is willing to teach what they know and LEARN from them. Finally, they DO what they have learned. Pretty simple. Except in my life, I started at the wrong step. I LEARNED (got an Engineering degree), I DID what an engineer did when I went to work, and I DEFINED my lifestyle based on what somebody else thought I was worth. I know it's crazy, but I didn't know any better. That's why I wasn't getting the results in life I wanted. Orrin Woodward was. I asked Orrin for help and he introduced me to the Team. I followed his advice and we have never looked back. I just wish I could have discovered someone like Orrin when I was 18 years old!

The Team is an extraordinary leadership training system. I'd stack it up against any corporate leadership training in the world. Because of our relationship with the Team and the Woodwards, my wife and I will never again have to fight rush hour traffic. We don't have to spend the best hours of our day at work with people we don't necessarily like and we don't have to spend any time doing things at work that we don't want to do.

People ask me why I would give up big money like $3,000/day as a consultant to build this business. My response is simple. First, I have a new definition of what big money is and $3,000/day is not it. Second, even though I was making decent money, I had to be there in order to be paid. I had the classic "S" (self-employment) business that Robert Kiyosaki discusses in his book. As I studied the business plan and looked at Orrin's commitment, I realized this was my way out of the "time-for-money" trap.

I realized the Team was something special when about six months into the business I was recognized on stage for accomplishing a certain level. I spoke for a couple of minutes and when I was done my son gave me a big hug and said, "Papa, I'm proud of you." No amount of money in the world can replace that special moment. I decided to build this business and give others a chance to win in life. I just wanted to give others a chance to feel the way I did.

If you currently own a business or ever thought of owning a business, here's the first thing you should do. Go to an Open Meeting. Second, meet the Team you'll be working with and find someone you relate with. Third, become familiar with the Team leadership training system. Don't use lack of time as an excuse not to do this, because you know it won't change – you'll never have enough time unless you do something different. Fourth, begin with the end in mind. What goal or dream have you been putting on the backburner due to lack of opportunity? Step out of the stands, get on the field, and take your swing. Wayne Gretzky said, "I miss 100% of the shots I don't take." I missed too many shots in my life, and I wasn't letting this one go.

The concept of freedom is hard to imagine when you're not free. It's like a permanent vacation, but with a purpose. And most people miss this: Freedom is not free. It must be *earned*. We earned our freedom through serving others. Like so many of the other Team leaders, we discovered that true happiness comes through helping others find their purpose.

"Thinking is the hardest work there is, that's why so few people
engage in it."
- Henry Ford

"If you think you can, you can. If you think you can't, you can't.
Either way, you're right."
- Mary Kay Ash

"Enough experience will make you wise."
- James R. Cook

"It is better to be wise than to seem wise."
- Origen (c. 185-254 A.D.)

"Isn't it splendid to think of all the things there are to find out
about?"
- Lucy Montgomery

Name: **SELFISH SAM**

Quote: "So how much can I make? Really!? Is there some way we can set it up so my wife can't get any of it?"

Chapter 3

Power Player
The Only Play Necessary

Having a burning desire or dream is the most important step toward success. But once you've clearly established what you want, and begun the journey of learning the correct thinking, it's time for action. With the Team business, we each have an opportunity equally matched to our dreams, and we have something we can "do" to make those dreams come true.

First Steps

An athlete showing up to training camp starts with some basic orientation, followed by stretches and warm-ups. If you are brand new to the Team business, there are a couple of early steps we highly recommend you take to get yourself acclimated to the business. Consider them to be stretches and warm-ups.

First and foremost, attend an *Open Meeting* in your area. At the same time, we recommend that if you haven't already, begin by thoroughly reviewing the material in the *First-Night Pack* and the *Additional Information Pack*. There are no more important steps to take to begin understanding the business.

Next, review any of the materials concerning *How to Get Started*. This information represents the most basic and detailed "How To" training. It presents the basic fundamental steps to building a large and profitable business. Consider these to be as critical as proper blocking and tackling in football. Without a firm knowledge base in these areas, no fancy playbook in the world could be expected to work.

Also, if you're reading this book you are on the right track. Finally, we recommend you clear your schedule and attend the next *Seminar* or *Major Convention* that becomes available.

Success begins with information from the right source, and by plugging into the Team training system of meetings and materials (called "tools"), as just described, you are doing just that!

Systematic Success

Ray Kroc, the founder of McDonald's, took the business of franchising out of the dark ages and into the modern era. He fundamentally changed it in order to make it work. What was once thought to be a scam and probably even illegal has become a staple of American retailing. The principle behind the success of Kroc's strategy is this: business runs on ability and knowledge. Those with the ability and knowledge have the success. Those without it, don't, plain and simple. Kroc systematized the *sharing* of best-practices and business wisdom *from* the successful *to* the hopeful. A new business owner could know nothing about business, franchising, or restaurants, but could buy into McDonald's and learn it all. As the restaurant owner grew his business and prospered, so too would the parent company for sharing their expertise.

Ray Kroc bought something called the "McDonald's System" from the founding McDonald brothers in California. Their "system" was a finely detailed method of operating their store that was proven to bring profits. Success was not left to chance; it was "systematized." This system is readily apparent when simply walking into a McDonald's restaurant. The menu is above the counter, the fry machine is to the left, the bathrooms are to the right, and the children's play area is right out front. And these are just the obvious details. Bookkeeping, inventory management, staffing, and inspections are all regimented and systematic. The McDonald's system works so well, nearly every restaurant in North America makes money each year!

In the Team business (thankfully), we have no restaurant or facility. We have no inventory or cleanliness inspections. We have no playground. But we *do* have proven best-practices that work in our industry. We *do* have a systematic, proven approach to financial success. That systematic approach is called the Power Player Program, and business owners who fully utilize Power Player to build their businesses experience consistent success.

McDonald's sells its expertise to new restaurant owners and then places enormous control over each store's operation. The Team makes the Power Player Program available to all its business owners, but exerts no control over its implementation. This is where the Team business parts ways with franchising. Where franchises exert control, the Team exerts none. Where franchises take the credit for their people's success, the Team will not. But where franchising shares best-practices and proven business strategies to produce duplicatable, systematic success, the Team runs with the best of them.

The Play

We love sports. Athletic competitions embody the success principles that are required to succeed in life in nearly any field. Sports represent the classic struggles of man against man, army against army, and man against himself. We must confess; football is a favorite. We like the contact, the strategy, the heroic catches and last second finishes.

Imagine a football team that couldn't be stopped: a team with an offensive play that scored every time. The players break huddle and get into position along the line of scrimmage. The quarterback barks out the signals and the center snaps the ball. All the blocking works perfectly and the play scores, *every time!* Can you even imagine such a thing?

With the Team business, there is actually such a play. The business owner goes up to the line and barks out the play, "Power Player!" Everybody knows it is the play that will be called. It is the same play he called on the previous drive. It's the same play he called in last week's game, and all of last season. But it scores every time! It has never been stopped.

"Power Player" is an all-encompassing business building program with a proven track record. In fact, it has worked so well year after year, that we keep on calling the same play over and over. Those that use it and execute it properly have growing businesses, repeatedly and predictably.

The point is that the business is 100% predictable. It is not a "does it work" business. It is a "do you work it" business. If you do the work, it will work. If you follow the proven pattern, if you call the Power Player play, if you stay consistent, the results are extremely predictable.

Please notice that we didn't say it was easy. We didn't say it was something for nothing. We didn't say it was guaranteed, because nothing in life is. But it is predictable. You can expect reasonable results for the right amount of consistent, correct inputs. Continue those inputs according to the Power Player strategy, and the results crescendo and grow to larger and larger levels. Soon what you once thought of as "good money" doesn't seem so "good" any more. What you once thought of as a "good job" might not seem so "good" anymore. Gradually and consistently, you will be growing in financial ability and will start "checking off" dreams along the way. All this and more can happen because of a little concept called Power Player.

The Playbook

Every football team has a playbook that details each of their plays. The playbooks are a valuable source of knowledge for the players because, in effect, the playbook says, "This is how we do it here."

What do you think the value of an NFL football team's playbook would be? How about one from a team that had just won the Super Bowl? What if a team had won Super Bowls year after year? Would you say that they had something going for them? Would you say that they had something consistent that they were doing that brought such unprecedented success?

The Team's playbook, which has helped us place among the fastest growing teams in the industry for years running, is actually not a book at all! It's a simple concept called *The Power Player Program*. This program, in a very concise way, encompasses the key features of building the business and tracking progress. This program provides the framework for a business owner to quickly learn "how we do it here."

The Program

The Power Player Program is broken down into three main areas:

1. Theory
2. Activity
3. Results

Theory is important because "you don't know what you don't know." And this is particularly true when it comes to this business. One may be a successful professional, a small business owner or a teacher; one may have succeeded financially before or have obtained a top-notch education, but that doesn't make him an expert here. This is a whole new ball game. Certainly the life skills obtained in other occupations, such as people skills, goal setting and continuing education, can be useful in this business. But there is a specific body of material that must be mastered in order for the business owner to know what to do, how to do it, and how to duplicate it. One of the best ways to learn is through experience – that is, experience of those who have been successful. That's what the *theory* part of the business provides.

Activity is critical because all the theory in the world is useless unless it is applied to something. Learning should not lead to knowledge, it should lead to action.

Finally, a focus on *results* is paramount because without working toward something specific, and without following an exact strategy, the business owner can learn a lot, do a lot, but not accomplish a lot. Success is not knowledge. Success is not being busy. Success is getting results.

The Power Player Program embodies all three of these areas and breaks them down into manageable parts. The chapters to follow will explore each of these areas more closely.

Training Camp

The purpose of this discussion on the Power Player Program is to let you know that there is a path for you to follow. There is a road map to the place where your goals and dreams can come true. You will use the Power Player Program the rest of your career as a business owner, and it is *the thing* that you should work on mastering as you become more and more active in building your business. But we run the risk of giving you information flow that may make you feel as if you are drinking from a fire hose!

The Power Player Program in its entirety may be a bit much to swallow in your very first days in the business. Don't try to master it all at once. Professional football players may be given their team's playbook at the beginning of training camp, but they have a while to memorize it and learn how to execute each of its plays. The same will be true of the new Team business owner. It is important to understand that **Power Players embody the ultimate business building characteristics.** Steve Sabol of NFL films said, "Good players turn up at the right time or the right place, or do the right things. Great players do all three." In this business, the "great" players are the Power Players. Power Players learn the right things, apply them properly, and focus upon and achieve the right results.

It may take a little while to build up to the point where you can plug into each of the steps involved with this program. Nobody will push you to be more involved than you can or want to be. Remember, you are in your own business. You are free to build it as fast or slow as you want or need. You will be *encouraged* to pursue the entire Power Player Program as soon as you are ready or able, but ultimately, the decision on how to proceed and how fast to go are up to you. The last thing in the world we want is for someone to review the Power Player Program and get "overwhelmed." Anything can appear to be complicated or cumbersome when looked upon for the first time or by somebody unfamiliar with the industry. But as time passes and one gets more familiar with the business and its details, it becomes obvious that this business is quite simple. We build communities of people through which products and services flow, online, and we follow a proven pattern and system to make that happen. The Power Player Program organizes the steps required to make that happen into their simplest form. We recommend that you look at your first several months in the business as your training camp. Take everything in. Learn all that you can. Ask questions and be a sponge for information and knowledge about success. And most importantly, have fun! Becoming a business owner is one of the most exciting and rewarding things you can do, and even more so with the Team business. So enjoy the process of learning and getting up to speed. Welcome to training camp!

Personal Stories

Name: Bill and Jackie Lewis

Former Occupations: Engineer; Self-Employed Contractor

I was introduced to the Team by a co-worker while I was an engineer. I was looking for something different but was still skeptical about what he was going to show me. After I saw the business plan, I immediately knew it would work because it made too much sense.

I really understood and saw the business for what it was after I went to a "Major Function." I saw people that looked just like me and were having success. I saw people that said how this business had changed their life because of the mentorship and the success system they were using. I saw a way to get my goals and dreams. I was sold out. When I arrived home, I immediately started to build the business.

As I learned to listen to CD's, read books, and attend the events, my thinking got better and better and my business results followed. Things seemed easy at first, but then I started to hit some challenges. My mentor, Mark, helped me through those times. He was always there for me. I remember many times when he encouraged me and told me that I could do it. Rarely in my life had I ever had anyone who was in my corner like that. Growing up on the streets of a tough town, you don't always get encouragement from your friends (If you do, it's encouragement to do some pretty crazy things!) But Mark became my great encourager. It's what our system teaches us all to do for each other.

I'll never forget the time when I had almost given up on myself. No matter what I did it seemed I couldn't move this business ahead. I started to listen to the negative doubts inside that were telling me I couldn't do this. "This isn't going to work!" I thought. "Not for me." And I came as close as ever to just throwing in the towel and quitting altogether. I had reached my lowest point of belief in myself and my ability to build the business. I'll never forget that night. There I was driving alone in the dark, about to quit

42

on my dreams. But just at that moment, like a dart in the darkness, my cell phone rang. It was Mark. He had called just to check up on me and tell me he believed in me. He was proud of my efforts and knew I could make it. I had tears in my eyes when I hung up. How could I quit? How could I give up on myself when my mentor believed in me and cared for me so much? I would never quit. Never. I was going to make it! Mark had snatched me back from the jaws of mediocrity and self pity.

A little while later I was able to leave my job, and have since seen many of my friends that I brought into the business do the same. We are living a free lifestyle. We are a squad of business owner/friends that love building this business and helping other people. And I owe it all to my mentors Mark, Chris, and Orrin. They and their wives have each been there to help me through some pretty big growth opportunities. This is what makes the Team special. It doesn't matter where you come from or what you have done before. If you are hungry and willing to be mentored, you can have success here.

I know, because it happened for me.

Name: Kirk and Cassie Birtles
Former Occupations: Physical Therapist; Secretary

I was a shy, small-town, 26 year old when I graduated with my Masters degree in Physical Therapy. Through eight years of college, deferred gratification had been my means of survival. I was a broke student who always had a bunch of roommates and a dump of a place. I drove a 1986 Mercury Grand Marquis and could fit all of my worldly possessions in its trunk. I lived on macaroni and cheese, pizza rolls, and sub sandwiches. After jumping through all the hoops and loops of my 125 credit masters program, I had my degree, and thought, "You did it! Life is now going to get good."

I was wrong. I ended up with a student loan payment of $700.00 a month for 30 years. Now I was a broke professional, who still ate sub sandwiches and frozen pizza, still had a roommate, but now had less free time because I had to work so much to pay my bills. All I had to show for my eight years of effort was a $100,000 piece of paper and a 60 hours-a-week job. I was frantically trying to figure out what I could do to change my seemingly inevitable future of no time, no money and total mediocrity. I wasn't "institutionalized" yet, like so many co-workers, friends and family that had already given up hope for a better tomorrow, but I was well on my way. I didn't want to settle for a life full of weekend-warrior sports and softball leagues, reality TV and sports news. I was unhappy, unchallenged, and felt as though something was missing in my life. I had always felt that I was going to do something great, but for some reason I got off on the wrong exit of life and did not know what to do next.

I had been out of college for one year when a co-worker and friend started to talk to me about the Team. At first, my friend had no enthusiasm at all about the Team and I really didn't take the time to listen. Then he attended a Team "Major Function" and came back so excited that I had to take a look at what the Team had to offer. My eventual sponsor convinced me, through his excitement and conviction, to skip one of my softball league games. He drove me to a Team Open Meeting about two hours away. That meeting was a truly magical event for me. When it was over, I had hope and excitement back in my life! I was a little unsure whether someone like me could succeed with the Team, but I was more excited than anything. I kept thinking, "What if this works? What if I can get out of debt? What if I can get out my job?" From there, my now friend and mentor, Aron, lead the way and gave me a great example to follow. Cassie, my fiancé at the time, saw the plan from Aron and has been my wonderful partner ever since.

Our true "light bulb" moment, where we really believed we could go all the way with the Team, was the first time we achieved Power Player. It really convinced us that we could build this business and succeed at it. Since that first time going Power Player, we have sold out to the Power Player/ Turbo program and have been on a quest to get better and do more every day.

Performing within the Team business has allowed us to pay off close to 6 figures of high interest credit card and consumer debt, and has allowed us to replace our incomes and become full time parents for our three blessed children. This business has given us hope, purpose, and the means to make a difference in millions of peoples lives. We have only just begun our journey with the greatest leadership team in the world, but we know in our heart of hearts, God willing, that we will follow the leadership of the Team and the principles they stand for to the four corners of the world!

"The most beautiful thing in the world is the conjunction of learning and inspiration."
- Wanda Landowski

"It's not how much time you put into something that counts. It's what you put into the time that counts."
- unknown

"We can't take any credit for our talents. It's how we use them that counts."
- Madeleine L'Engle

"When you convert ideas into action you are seldom disappointed."
- Alexander Lockhart

"A man is not old until his regrets take the place of his dreams."
- John Barrymore

Name: SUSIE STATUS

Quote: "Are there any famous people in this? We have a reputation in this community and I'm not sure we could tell our friends about this unless there are famous people involved."

Chapter 4

Theory
Tools, Meetings, and Subscriptions

The best way to begin your business is with a good attitude, and the most important attitude to have is that of a *student*. Many people come into the business with a critical eye; they pass judgment on everything they are told and everything that takes place and think they know how and what they should be taught to succeed. But as Diamond Business Owner, Tim Marks says, "This business doesn't necessarily build the way you might think it does." Therefore, begin your business as a *student* and not as a *critic*.

Learning is one of life's biggest blessings. It can and should be fun and rewarding. These truths are more relevant when the learning is in an area about which the individual is enthusiastic. The more excited one is about building his or her business, the more fun and the faster the learning will be. Realize that successful people are hungry learners. In our book, *Launching a Leadership Revolution,* we dedicated a whole chapter to the concept of learning as the first rung on the ladder to leadership greatness. This is because without the attitude of a student, and without the understanding that there is always something more to learn, an individual will be limited in his or her accomplishments. One never arrives. One never gets to the place where he or she has it "all figured out." There is *always* more to learn.

Another important component of success is learning from those who have succeeded themselves. Everybody has an opinion; all that's required is a mouth that works! But that doesn't mean those opinions have any validity for achievement. *Success begins with information from the correct source.* In other words, be careful from whom you learn, they might not have the results you want! If you listen to broke people about finances, chances are you'll pick up their habits and end up with their financial situa-

49

tion. If you listen to those who are wealthy, your chances of becoming wealthy skyrocket.

The Power Player Program organizes the learning that is required to build the Team business. It teaches both principles and specifics, and it is taught by those who have achieved success in the Team business. The program is designed to fit the lifestyles of most people who are too busy to attend classroom instruction and can't afford expensive tuitions, and it follows the pattern of learning recommended by so many of the world's most successful. As co-author of the wildly popular *Chicken Soup for the Soul* series, Mark Victor Hansen says, "Read books, listen to tapes, attend seminars – they are decades of wisdom reduced to invaluable hours." Additionally, the learning associated with Team, through the Power Player Program, is financially affordable and flexible in your schedule.

The educational steps involved in the *theory* portion of the Power Player Program are:

1. Subscribe to CD's of the Week
2. Subscribe to Book of the Month
3. Subscribe to Standing Order Leadership CD
4. Purchase a Top 50 CD Set
5. Attend Open Meetings and Night Owls
6. Attend Men's or Ladies' Leaderships
7. Attend Seminars
8. Attend Major Functions
9. Subscribe to Website
10. Subscribe to Voice Mail system

To be recognized as a Power Player, each of these ten aspects of the "Theory" portion of the program must be fulfilled by the business owner (as well as the aspects of the "Activity" and "Results" categories to be explained in subsequent chapters). Again, a Power Player is a big accomplishment. He or she represents an inner circle of achievers on the Team. Power Players receive special recognition, have special meetings and training focuses, and are provided special seating at the national conventions. Don't panic if you don't think you can do all of these steps right away. Just work towards them, and know the rewards for Power Player will be well worth it, in many ways!

CD's of the Week

A wealth of information can be gained through what might be called "passive learning." This is learning that takes place easily while one is doing something else, such as driving to work or completing chores. Audio recordings are one of the best sources of passive learning. Author Brian Tracy said that if one listens to experts in a given field for thirty minutes a day, in just a year that person will be as informed as anyone on the topic, and an expert within another year. The authors have no way to verify the timeline of this claim but know it to be true in spirit. That's because it worked for us. We were both in poor financial condition when someone introduced an audio training program to us. Without that training, we would not be where we are today, period! Without a doubt!

Audio recordings in the form of compact discs (CD's) are an extremely convenient, portable source of education. In the Team's training system, the CD's are recordings of speeches or training sessions given by leaders in the business. Each speaker featured on a CD has attained a leadership level on the Team, and has proven his or her ability to grow this business. This is where the value of the CD's comes in – the information contained therein. "I can buy blank CD's at the store for forty cents," someone might say. "Yes," we could reply, "but listening to them will produce no financial results in your life. They are blank! It's not the CD itself, but the information that is important." It's the information that makes the Team CD's so valuable. And it is information with a proven track record.

The CD's of the Week program is designed to build expertise on the part of the business owner over a consistent period of time. On a weekly basis, the subscribing business owner receives two CD's, the latest released title from each of two series. One series focuses primarily on expository teaching, the other on teaching through story and example. Each recording is brand new, usually selected from training sessions and seminars and other talks given around the western hemisphere to the Team audiences. Occasionally, outside talks are selected if they are found to be world-class and relevant to the building of the Team business.

The *weekly* nature of the CD's of the *Week* program has proven to be critical. This is for several very important reasons. First, most people do not join the Team business with what could be called "wealth-thinking." (Even in the remote cases where someone has experienced personal financial expertise and the corresponding success, it is still necessary to obtain specifics of the Team business.) We need to be "un-educated" on all the incorrect things we have learned over the years about money, success, and accomplishment. Secondly, we receive a large amount of friction, negative input, and abrasion on a *daily* basis, whether in the workforce, at home, or around friends and family. So there is a combined need to "undo" all the cumulative wrong that has been programmed into our brains, and also to combat the new negative on an ongoing basis. For these reasons, like an antibiotic fighting off a germ, the CD's of the Week program provides a consistent dosage. There is also an entertainment factor to the CD's that is hard to quantify: they are fun to listen to. Most people find they have a better attitude when regularly listening to Team CD's. After all, it's just good food for the soul to hear positive, uplifting, and encouraging words in a world normally full of cynicism and hurt.

Power Players are enthusiastically involved with the CD's of the Week program.

Book of the Month

The Book of the Month program is designed to teach in an entirely different fashion than the CD's of the Week do. First of all, reading brings information into our brain in a different way than listening to an audio recording does. While an audio recording is in the voice of whoever is speaking, when we read a book we hear the words in our own voice. Additionally, our brain processes written information differently. It is more organized, classified, and tabulated than the audio variety.

Many people are visual learners and find reading to be a natural thing. Others prefer audio learning and find CD's to be the easiest from which to learn. *Both* are comprised in the Power Player Program because everyone can learn from both, no matter what his or her preference. The two learning styles together make a great combination. One (CD's) allow for passive learning, the other (books) give organized, active learning.

"But I haven't read a book since high school," one might say. "I hate to read," says another. We understand. We know how you feel. As a matter of fact, we felt the same way. But here's what we found: once we started reading the books in this business, and began learning about things that were *directly relevant* to getting our goals and dreams, we found that we were actually *enjoying* reading!

Reading is one of the biggest secrets to success in general, and certainly so in this business. To quote our book, *Launching a Leadership Revolution:*

> It is a fact that most of the greatest leaders throughout history have been avid readers. Napoleon as a young boy read books constantly. President Teddy Roosevelt was known to read at least a book a day, and sometimes two, even while President! Thomas Jefferson bought books compulsively throughout his life and read them with even more vigor than he collected them. Singer and songwriter Jimmy Buffett said of his mother, "She taught me that reading is the key to everything."
>
> Books represent the accumulated knowledge and wisdom of the ages, available for pennies on the dollar. Books preserve the greatest thoughts, the greatest ideas, and the greatest insights of human experience. Roy L. Smith said, "A good book contains more wealth than a good bank." Reading a book puts one in touch with an author the reader may never have a chance to meet in person, either because of distance or time. And reading is one of

the best, most time-tested avenues to leadership experience. If other people's experience is the best teacher, books are the best transmitter of that experience. True leaders know this and make reading a consistent part of their plan for success. Jim Rohm said, "If you read a book a week, in a year you'll have read 52 books. In ten years 520 books. You'll be in the top 1% of your field. You'll be more motivated, better educated; you'll become the leader in your field." Charles Scribner, Jr. said, "Reading is a means of thinking with another person's mind: It forces you to stretch your own." William J. O'Neil, founder of *Investor's Business Daily,* said ". . . people who hope to successfully influence what goes on around them will develop the habit of reading great books." Ralph Waldo Emerson said, "Many times the reading of a book has made the future of a man."

Sometimes, when we tout the benefits of reading, people assume we mean reading for entertainment. "Oh good!" they say, "I already read several novels a month." Certainly there is an entertainment value to reading. But when we speak of reading good books, we are not referring to the latest dime-store thriller that keeps one turning pages or to the type of books that can be "read in one sitting." As the evangelist and writer A.W. Tozer said, "The best book is the one that sets us off on a train of thought that carries us far away from and far beyond the book itself." Our reading should be guided by our need and desire to grow as leaders; fashioning us into better people. Our reading should not just be for enjoyment, but should foster growth in our minds and persons. Reading should lead to better thoughts, which in turn lead to better actions, which then lead to better habits, which then produce better results, which then produce a better future.

From leaders like George Washington, Thomas Jefferson, Abraham Lincoln, Theodore Roosevelt and Harry Truman, to writers like Ralph Waldo Emerson, Henry David Thoreau and Ernest Hemingway, to entertainers like Oprah Winfrey, Jimmy Buffett and Woody Allen, to historical figures like Socrates, Diderot, Gustave Flaubert and Francis Bacon, leaders are encouraged over and over to make reading a regular part of their diet. As perhaps only Mark Twain could say, "The man who does not read good books has no advantage over the man who can't read them."

We couldn't avoid this lengthy quotation because we feel so strongly about the power of reading (and we couldn't have written that section any better than we did the first time)! The Book of the Month program feeds this very important aspect of success and is the backbone of personal growth and achievement.

All Power Players subscribe to the Book of the Month program.

Standing Order Leadership CD

Power Players are leaders. They want to learn all they can. They are hungry for the information that will help them move on. The Standing Order Leadership CD series is a one CD per week hard-core, no-fluff, leadership training format designed to give the business owner *leadership* information. This is information that only has relevance if the business owner understands the fundamentals of the business. For this reason, Standing Order Leadership is only available to those business owners who are plugged into the CD's of the Week Program. Leadership recordings are taken from leadership training sessions, only. So be careful. Leadership CD's are not for the feint of heart. Listening to them just might produce radically positive changes in your life and finances!

All Power Players subscribe to the Standing Order Leadership CD's.

Top 50 CD Set

Throughout the years, the Team has produced numerous recordings that have gained widespread popularity among business owners for their teaching content, specific strategies, principles, or sheer motivational value. The Top 50 CD Set is a compilation of the "best of the best" recordings produced in the Team's history. And let us tell you, it is not an easy list to assemble! Narrowing down the vast list of recordings to just 50 is nearly impossible. Discussion about which CD's make it into the list can go on for hours and hours, with input from leaders throughout the top levels of the organization fighting it out and calling each other names! Okay, not really. But there is a lot of wringing of hands and gnashing of teeth. Not a pretty sight. So you can imagine the potency of the 50 CD's that are left standing after all of this! These 50 CD's are the absolute best the Team has to offer to a business owner for building his or her business.

The Top 50 CD set comes in a black box. The intent is that the Top 50 will be the business owner's personal library on success. Its information is indestructible, just like the "black box" recorders used in commercial airliners. When a plane crashes, the black box is always recovered in working order (which makes one wonder why they don't make the entire plane out of that black box material). The Top 50 CD's should be listened to again and again. It could even be said that the better a business owner knows his Top 50, the better he knows his business.

There have been examples where somebody was sponsored into the business at a distance from any other significant Team activity, and had access to the training system primarily through the Top 50 CD set. Armed solely with this information, they were able to build the business successfully. This is because so much information is encompassed by the teaching in that little black box!

Power Players own their own black box, and they learn from it on a regular basis.

Open Meetings

One of the most critical components of the Team's training system is "Open Meetings." Open Meetings, or "Opens," as they are often called, are actually not "open." Rather, they are "invite only." But they are "open" to any business owner on the Team and any guests he or she would care to bring along.

The purpose of Open Meetings is to provide an introductory environment for new people to check out the Team business opportunity. The first part of the meeting concentrates on "showing the plan" (described in depth in Chapter 6). Here, the business opportunity is drawn out in detail by someone already succeeding at building the business. This can be considered as the "what it is" part of the meeting. The second part of the meeting focuses on teaching the new or prospective business owners how to actually begin building the business for themselves. This can be considered as the "how to do it" part of the meeting.

Attending Open Meetings is important for several reasons. First, Opens are intended to introduce new people to the business. As a business owner exposes people to the program, the Open Meetings are there to give the prospect a "second look." Second, Opens provide the business owner with a picture of the proper way to present the business, or "show the plan." One of the best ways to learn is through repetition. Week after week, as the business owner sees the plan drawn out by different leaders, he increases his own ability to explain the program. Third, Open Meetings are a chance for the business owner to associate with his or her team and up-line, and build the relationships that are so key to the business. Fourth, the "Night Owl," or second portion of the meeting, focuses mainly on the What, Why, and How of becoming a Power Player. So Opens are a main source of training for business owners that want their business to grow fast and profitably. Fifth, Open Meetings are very exciting. They are an excellent source of motivation and can help keep the business owner focused and consistent, much as the CD's of the Week program is designed to do. Some business owners have told us they can't wait for Tuesday night to roll around so they can get their weekly dose of "positive" in an otherwise negative world.

Power Players attend all weekly Open Meetings and Night Owls.

Men's or Ladies' Leadership Meetings

On a semi-regular schedule, (which changes at the whim of the Policy Council and with the training needs of the organization), both Men's and Ladies' Leadership Meetings are offered. These extremely popular meetings provide training along lines that are gender-specific. These events always feature speakers from the highest levels of the Team, and are designed to be very specific about issues facing each gender in their efforts to build the business. What should a single lady do to build the business? How does a married couple build the business? What do I do if my spouse is not all that interested in building the business with me? How do my spouse and I become more effective business partners in this deal? These and more are the kinds of questions and issues addressed at the Men's and Ladies' Leadership Meetings.

Power Players attend all such leadership meetings (within the qualifications of their gender, of course).

Monthly Seminars

Seminars are held monthly at locations across the country and can vary in size from a couple hundred attendees to thousands upon thousands, depending upon the area. The Team seminar system is designed to teach the What, Why and How of building the business. This training picks up where the weekly Night Owls leave off. The teaching is both expository (explained), and demonstrated (through personal stories), and therefore reaches across all varieties of learning styles in the audience. Ask any big leaders on the Team, and they will say that the Seminars have been critical to their success. Seminars are also an excellent opportunity to recognize achievers for their performance in the preceding month, and this is done for varying levels throughout the program.

These events are ticketed in advance, much like a sporting event (but much more valuable to the attendee!). A program called Standing Order Tickets has been developed for the convenience of the business owner. In this program, tickets are distributed well in advance of the scheduled seminar. This provides the business owner with an opportunity to have her seminar tickets in hand as she shares the business plan with others. This makes them available to be passed along to the prospective business owner as a way to begin their training, or to get a deeper look at the Team business. The power of this convenience will become more apparent as the reader reaches later chapters in this book. Suffice it to say that Power Players are on the Standing Order Ticket program because it helps them build their business faster! All Power Players attend the monthly Seminars and subscribe to Standing Order Ticket.

Major Functions

Major functions are the grand daddy's of the entire Team training system. They are the crème de la crème, the cake under the icing, the ice burg under the tip, the ponies under the hood, the . . . you get the idea. Major functions are national conventions that provide the chance for business owners throughout a large geographic region to gather and learn from the Team's national top leaders. At Majors, higher level recognition is showcased, business building competition winners are awarded, and an overall arrangement of topics and speakers comprising information from every aspect of building the business are presented. Major functions are the culmination of months of business growth through the Open Meetings and local monthly Seminars. Majors comprise two days worth of training, and even offer special meetings available only to Power Players, or other high level achievers.

For many reasons, Major Functions are the most important events of the year. Nearly every leader on the team can trace his or her decision to build the business back to something that was said or happened at a Major Function. As is commonly said, "Decisions are made at Major Functions." One of the reasons for this is that business owners tend to get the "big picture" at Major Functions. The experience might be analogous to attending a live concert versus listening to the same recording artist on CD. There is just something magical about being on location with all our senses taking in everything that happens. The amount of informa-

tion and perspective is so comprehensive, in fact, nearly over-
whelming, that people understand just how big this business is
and where it is heading. That understanding leads to belief.
Belief leads to results, and that's the reason to attend in the first
place – to obtain results!

Power Players attend the Major Functions, because they generate results like no other event!

* * *

The purpose of the Team training meetings just discussed
(Opens, Seminars, Leaderships, and Major Functions) is to provide
association with successful people. To paraphrase author Robert
Kiyosaki, our income will probably be somewhere in the ballpark
of the people we hang around the most. More importantly, we have
discovered that the best experience is somebody else's. The various meetings provide the opportunity to associate with those who
have experience and success that we can utilize to shorten our
journey and increase our wealth-thinking. For most of us, finding
someone who is financially successful, and who is willing to teach
us how they accomplished it, is next to impossible. If we *do* happen to know somebody who has succeeded to the financial levels
we desire, he or she usually has no motivation to share that experience with us. The meetings of the Team training system formal-
ize that association and sharing of experience to the benefit of all
who attend. As Kiyosaki stated in *The Business School,* "One of
the beauties of network marketing is that it gives you the opportunity to face your fears, deal with your fears, overcome your fears,
and let the winner in you win. To me, learning to sell, learning to
overcome my fear of rejection and learning to get my point across
is the best education I have ever received." The Team's system,
and especially its meetings, provides just that kind of education
and environment.

Subscribe to the Website

Through the years, the Team has come to rely more and more

upon its central form of communication: the website. What began as a great place to share basic announcements and information has blossomed into a centralized communication tool. Promotions of new events and training aids, answers to frequently asked questions, articles on growing volume and building the business bigger, comics, humor articles, e-mail, recognition, contest explanations, photo and video galleries, training aid ordering and payment, business tracking, famous quotes, mission and purpose statements, business histories, leader profiles, and many other features now comprise this enormous hub of business information. Clearly, we could not do business without it.

Need to know where the closest Open Meeting is in your area? Check the website. Who is speaking at the upcoming monthly Seminar? Check the website. Who won the latest promotion? Check the website. You get the idea.

As time passes and the business continues to grow, the Team will be incorporating more features into the website to make it even more interactive and valuable as a training and information source. The Team does not believe in utilizing technology for technology's sake, but it does pursue every avenue of advantage that can be gleaned from data management and presentation, information sharing and flow, and communication of every type. The Team has made a commitment to be a *world-class* organization, and massive investments have and are continually made to maximize the advantages a highly functional web-interface can provide.

Power Players subscribe to the website and use it to its fullest.

Subscribe to the Communication Systems

Piggybacked with the website is the Team's voice mail and e-mail system. This centralized electronic message system allows business owners to communicate with other business owners, both up-line and in their group. It minimizes interruptions and allows users to communicate when it is convenient for *them*, twenty-four hours a day, seven days a week. There are also centralized messages sent out from the Team office announcing schedule improvements or changes, recognitions sent from up-line leaders, and basic instructions and trainings. Distribution lists are available to allow one message to access an entire list of individuals, allowing a business owner the ability to speak to entire sections, or all of his or her organizations with one message. These types of economies of time play a big role as one's business gets bigger and bigger, saving everybody a lot of time. This type of electronic communication also allows distance groups to stay well-connected to their up-line without long distance phone bills or cell phone charges.

For these and many other reasons, Power Players subscribe to all the relevant communication systems available to stay connected, to keep their people informed, and to build their businesses.

Summary

Power Players are not afraid of learning; as a matter of fact, they crave it. Power Players plug into the full line of training aids to maximize their learning and grow their effectiveness. They know that learning by listening and reading, then associating with others that have succeeded through the various meetings available, and finally communicating through the website and voice mail, is their fastest path to success.

"Theory" is required to help the business owner avoid the time-wasting process of trial-and-error. The fastest and safest path to success is in the footsteps of those who have succeeded before. The Team training system embodied by the Power Player Program does just that. It provides the path of knowledge to the place where dreams can come true.

Alas, there is no something for nothing. Knowledge and learning alone will not generate success. Although the training system provides a pathway of knowledge, that pathway must still be traversed. That brings us to the next section: activity.

Personal Story

Names: Matt and Cheryl Abraham
Former Occupations: Attorney; Teacher

It was late on a Friday evening, the light was beginning to fade and there I sat. My wife and son were home, waiting for me and the weekend to arrive. We would be celebrating his first birthday tomorrow. I wanted to be home with them but there at the office I sat. I had pushed my chair away from my desk far enough to rest my head upon it, closed my eyes and without thinking at all, I prayed, "There has to be another way." I was working too many hours, and I saw no way out.

After seven years of full-time undergraduate and graduate education, two degrees, eight years of full-time legal practice, six as a solo-practitioner with my own successful practice, hundreds of thousands of dollars spent to just get there, having married a beautiful wife, a great mother to my son, a masters educated teacher with a solid 5-figure income, HOW DID I GET HERE? Cheryl and I had built a new home maximizing our ability (credit) to leverage the bank's money; financed the carpet, the furniture, the window blinds and appliances; leased 2 cars we obviously could not afford, charged vacations, all for what?

I was now living my obligations instead of my priorities and was not sure when or how it happened. I thought I had done and even surpassed exactly what everyone said was necessary to be "successful" and yet here I was feeling stuck. The weight of the frustration and anger felt as if I might be crushed under it. It had now seemed as though for so long we unknowingly had pursued status instead of purpose, immediate gratification instead of long-term vision. Instead of pursuing what we truly wanted, we settled for what we could have in the moment. I seemed to now be living the words Henry David Thoreau spoke so long ago when he said that "most men lead lives of quiet desperation." I had no answers and knew no one else who had them either.

After the weekend of spending time with our families and

friends, I seemed to gain a perspective that clarified what I must do. I realized that if I was going to change our options, I was going to have to change something I was doing. But what? I had heard it said that when the pain of staying the same becomes greater than the pain of change... you'll change! Every night before going to bed I would go up to my son's room, sit on the edge of his bed and stroke his hair. As tears of feeling a failure ran down my face and under the pain of staying the same, I promised him that I would find a way. No matter what, I would find a way. And, thanks to my dad, I was and always had been a man of my word. I had just made a commitment to something that mattered most in my life and one that I *had* to keep.

I began to look. I looked at every opportunity that was readily and not so readily available to me. I considered becoming licensed as a real estate broker. I looked into constructing residential spec homes. A good friend and I researched becoming licensed to open insurance agencies across the state. Together, we looked into many things. He and I even negotiated the potential purchase of a vacation resort in eastern Africa. Yes, that Africa. We were considering every opportunity and spent long hours exploring the advantages and disadvantages of every single one of them. None seemed to be able to deliver the options we wanted. If I could just replace enough of Cheryl's income to get her home, even part-time, I could get my son out of daycare. If I could just find a way to be that hero to my son, I thought. Now, *there* was a true description of success.

After a year of searching and praying for anything that even appeared as if it could produce results, I had found nothing. Everything seemed to require more time and more money than I had to give. Trading time for dollars was like being in a tug-of-war where my family was always the loser falling into the mud. There was no way to produce more with less. My son then turned two, and I still had no answers.

Then it happened. My prayer was answered. A friend and business associate referred a gentleman to the insurance agent friend with whom I had been searching for other opportunities. He came in to get a homeowner's insurance policy for a 7-figure home he was buying. This guy, Orrin Woodward, was exactly my age, had a wife and four kids, had retired from his profession at the age of 31, and was living a lifestyle that most people could only dream of. In hearing Orrin describe where he was before developing his business, it sounded as if he was telling *my* story. He had done everything he was told was necessary for success and was at the top of his game in his profession, but had none of the options he wanted. Obviously, something had changed for him. He had done something about it. He had fought his way out. The question was "How", and I wasted no time asking it.

Man, I was looking.

When Orrin came back that next week to show me the business plan it was like someone had removed a thick layer of dry cracked mud from my eyes. In showing me Robert Kyosaki's *Cashflow Quadrant®,* Orrin literally drew me a picture of how Employees and Self-Employed people trade their most valuable resource, time, and trade it for a one-time payment of money. Once spent, it cannot be recovered, and there's only so much you can spend. It was painful to watch someone diagram my misery. He then explained how a 'B'-Type Business Owner did things differently by *investing* time in a system that produced compounded results. A *system.* It was what I'd been looking for without even knowing it. A system where even the most common man with a burning desire to succeed and the will to persevere could take advantage of what was happening in this new information age and carve out a slice of this massive wealth.

The part of the business that gave me the most belief at first was the team aspect. Orrin and Chris Brady had developed a Team Approach whereby more heads were better than one and a unified group of people could certainly accomplish more together than apart. I could see that this was more than just a pipe dream, it was a *pipeline* dream. This was a place where people had achieved significant results and were helping others to do the same. Initially, I was skeptical. This should not be surprising. After all, for the past eight years I had earned a living as a professional skeptic and was well paid to analyze businesses to determine whether they were advantageous to my clients or not. The only way I could find that this business could fail fell squarely upon me and my own performance, or lack thereof.

Orrin invited Cheryl and me to something called a seminar. Cheryl didn't even know what we were going to, but this event turned out to be the straw that broke the camel's back. We could not deny what we saw and felt. Barely into the second half, Cheryl leaned over and told me that she was not sure what this business was, or whether we would ever make any money doing it, but that she definitely wanted to be a part of it. The type of people that made up the Team, the type of thinking these people had, the professionalism and encouragement they displayed, revealed the character of the Team. We wanted in.

The rest is history that is still being written. We realized that in order to achieve the results we wanted, we had to learn what people with those results knew. Further, we had to learn to think the way they thought. And finally, we had to do what they did. Only then would we be able to achieve the results they had.

Two years after becoming an IBO affiliated with the Team and utilizing the Team System, we had built a business that replaced Cheryl's income and benefits. She retired at age 31 and came home to be with our two (now three) children full time: exactly as we had dreamed! Today, the business has replaced both of our incomes, and we have the freedom to spend more time with our three children in one day than we had spent before in a week. We have found a balance of faith, family, finance, friends and fitness.

We continue to build our business with a commitment to give to others what was given to us: a chance to change one's circumstances and determine one's destiny. This business is a chance to help others catch the rainbow's end and realize that the pot of gold resides within.

"It's what you learn after you know it all that counts."
- John Wooden

"What is defeat? Nothing but education; nothing but the first step to something better."
- Wendell Phillips

"The unexamined life is not worth living."
- Plato

"The next best thing to being clever is being able to quote someone who is."
- Mary Pettibone Poole

"Only the educated are free."
- Epictetus

"The only real ill-doing is the deprivation of knowledge."
- Plato

Name: BETTY BUSY-BODY

Quote: "Huh? Oh, go ahead I'm listening. You don't mind if I take care of a few things while you talk, do you?"

Chapter 5

Activity, Part One
Making the List and Contacting

Action is the handle that turns the crank on the machinery of theory, because sooner or later work is required to make one's dreams come true. As the anonymous saying states: "The superior man is modest in his speech but superior in his *actions*."

There are several parts involved in the activity portion of "building a community of people through which products and services flow." It is important to understand right up front that none of these are difficult in and of themselves. Each involves basic activities we have all done throughout our lives. Applying these basic functions to the Team business is what will be new to the beginning business owner, *new* but not *difficult*. This is truly one of the most exciting things about the Team business: the fact that *anybody* can do it. It doesn't require a certain education or background; one doesn't have to be "cerebral" or have a background in sales, and it won't involve learning to do things that only certain people have the talent to accomplish. The basic steps involved are achievable by *anyone*. Truly, anyone can build this business. It simply takes a decision to do the work.

It sometimes seems as though there is a "culture of complacency" in our society today. Somehow it has become acceptable to be average. Mediocrity is presented as "cool." Dissidence is presented as "artistic." But these are lies. They always have been, and they always will be.

Someone once asked us if the perils afflicting our society were due to ignorance or apathy. Our answer was that we didn't know and we didn't care!

Okay, we'll get serious.

Achievement, effort, personal growth, work, and pursuit of excellence are virtues; their opposites are *not*. There should be no shame in hard work; in fact, hard work should be a source of pride.

By pride, we don't mean the wrong kind of pride where one puts himself ahead of others and becomes boastful. By pride we mean "the self-satisfaction of knowing that you have given your very best to something, that indeed, you have tried your hardest." Think about it. When was the last time you *really* tried your *hardest* at something? Does your current job or profession require you to be *excellent*? Or can you just "get by?" Our bet is that many simply get by. In fact, there is a humorous saying that rings a little too true: "Companies will pay just enough to keep people from quitting, while people will do just enough to keep from getting fired." It doesn't have to be that way. Where true reward is available, true effort can be expended. That's what the Team business is all about: reward for performance. What the Team stands for, and what will be required to accomplish a dream lifestyle, is an individual or couple committed to accepting a challenge and giving it their best. Half-Throttle efforts produce half-throttle lifestyles. But real effort brings rewards immeasurable.

The activity of building the Team business consists of effort in two main areas:

1. Building a Community
2. Generating Product Flow

In one way or another, this entire book deals with Building a Community, while Generating Product Flow will be covered in Chapter 9.

Building a community is the key step. It's the task every great company must learn to achieve in order to have a loyal, continuing customer base. As we described earlier, Dell founder, Michael Dell, emphasized how developing a community of loyal, repeat buyers *online* is the key skill in today's new economy. It is this unique ability that the Team business provides and teaches. And it is this unique ability that sets us apart from the rest. Accomplishing the building of such a community, then, is of utmost importance. It should be *the thing* at which a new business owner focuses on becoming proficient. It is accomplished by using the Five Step Pattern, which involves:

70

1. Generating a list of names
2. Contacting
3. Showing the plan
4. Following through
5. Rotating the pattern – getting them started

As discussed above, these steps are very straight forward and simple to do. They involve activity anyone can do. Still, there are specifics to learn about each that will make the business owner the most effective. Remember, following proven patterns is a legitimate short-cut to success.

Generating a List of Names

Step number one in the Five Step Pattern is making a list of names. This seems almost too elementary to discuss. After all, who hasn't made a list before? Believe it or not, there are a few things to know in this step. There are some "best practices" that have proven to work very effectively.

The beginning business owner is encouraged to obtain a copy of the brochure, *Who Do You Know?* and to reference the *How to Get Started* materials.

The first thing to know about making a list of names of potential individuals to contact about the business is that this first step is a brainstorming exercise. The intent is to empty the brain entirely of every contact you have ever known. This doesn't mean you think they would all be good at the business or that you know how to get in touch with them. All you are trying to accomplish is a flow of names. By not prejudging any name that comes to mind, you free your brain to think of the next one. Hold nothing back. Have fun with it, and see how large you can make your initial list. Many times you may only remember a first name, or sometimes even less. You may simply know one as "the man who works at the accounting office." That's fine. Just find some way to record your recognition of that person and move on. The goal is to write down as many names as possible. All sorting and guessing who would

71

be most likely to respond positively to the business idea can come later.

The second thing to know about making a list of names is that it should be written. We have seen many, many people get started in the business and attempt to build it by keeping their names "in their head." Read carefully: *That doesn't work!* Feel free to verify it if you want, but you can save a lot of time by writing down a list of names from the very beginning of your business. "Why?" you might ask. We'll illustrate with a story, one that has recurred time and again in the Team's history. A person gets introduced to the business, gets involved and begins contacting people. But they never take the time to make a written list, so invariably they forget a few. They don't even realize it until they see one of those people at a Team event somewhere, involved with *somebody else!* "Why didn't you call me about this?" the person usually asks, to which there can be no good answer. "I forgot about you," isn't something anyone wants to hear! Don't make that mistake. Be a professional from the very start. Make a *written* list of names.

There is a strong tendency in the beginning for a business owner to prejudge people. For one reason or another people are left off the list or not considered as legitimate contacts. "They are rich already." "He would *never* do *this.*" "He wouldn't listen to me." "She's too busy." Again, let us give a warning: *Do not prejudge people.* Stories abound of big leaders on the team who were on somebody else's list but never contacted for reasons just like these. Then, those persons eventually joined the Team with somebody else and built the business big. Those are the kind of mistakes nobody wants to think about. The best way to avoid such an enormous loss of potential is to refrain from prejudging anybody and give them a chance to determine for themselves if they are interested in the business.

Once the names list is constructed, then it is a good idea to do two things with it. First, rearrange the names according to what might be called "affinity groups." These are groups of people that know each other already. Secondly, try to identify the most ambitious people on the list. There doesn't seem to be any "ideal" characteristic of one who will be most successful at this business, but there are four attributes common to the most successful business builders:

1. Ambitious
2. Looking for something more
3. Teachable
4. Honest

Whenever a person of this description is exposed to the business, he or she generally gets involved. Unfortunately, these characteristics are not easy to identify. At this point, simply make a guess. Some people *are* more ambitious than others. Some *are* looking for more in life. Some *are* more teachable than others. And finally, some *are* honest and some are not. Be careful not to turn this into prejudging, it is just a best-guess to where one should *begin*.

Throughout the years of building your business, the names list is to be a living, breathing document. It should be updated constantly, with new names and contacts added. It is a good idea to revisit this brainstorming exercise at least once a month to make sure you haven't forgotten anybody.

Contacting

A list of names is good, but by itself, it accomplishes nothing. We have seen people craft a beautiful list of names, but then do nothing with it. The purpose of generating a list of names in the first place is to get those names *off* that list, and that is accomplished through *contacting*.

Contacting is the initial connection to the business for the people on our list. It is very important, so much so, that many feel that as much as 50% of sponsoring a new business owner into the business depends on the contact. This is because it is the new person's first impression of the business. There are some great audio recordings contained in the *How to Get Started* materials that teach this step in detail.

The purpose of the contacting step is *not* to explain the business. It is *not* to convince people to join the business. It is not to tell them all about it. **The purpose of the contacting step is simply to *book an appointment*.** The reason for this is that the business cannot be properly portrayed by words. It must be drawn out. It must be given the explanation time that it deserves. The Team business is an enormous economic opportunity. It is right in the middle of the biggest business trends of our day. It has brought significant financial success to lots of people. For these reasons and more it is important to offer each prospect the business in a way that is the most relevant and as professional as possible. This is one of those points in the business where business owners just naturally mess it up. There is a tendency to explain the business or talk about it when all that is necessary is an appointment in the calendar. For that reason, allow us to reiterate: **The purpose of contacting is to book an appointment.**

How is this done? Again, too often business owners quickly go off track here. They think they know best how to contact their acquaintances and friends. But experience has shown that people, left to their own "knowledge," will do exactly the wrong thing just about every time. Remember, this business doesn't necessarily build the way you might think it builds. So make the decision early to follow proven strategies. It will save you a lot of time and anguish.

There are two types of events to which the contact will invite the prospect. The first is a "one-on-one" plan. The second is a "house plan." One-on-Ones involve one couple (or individual) talking to another couple (or individual). The second type of plan event is a house plan, where a gathering of prospects is arranged so the plan can be presented "en mass" on a white board. Depending upon which type of event to which the prospect is being invited, the guidelines for contacting may vary a little. Where this is the case, it will be explained accordingly. However, most of these principles of contacting are universal.

Let's talk about the principles first; then we'll get to the specifics.

Principles of Contacting

Be Brief

Do not get involved in a lengthy discussion or get to the point where the prospect is asking a string of questions and you are scrambling to answer them. Keep it short and simple. The best contact takes less than ninety seconds. As Tim Marks says, "Be bright, be brief, and be gone." Using a proven script, stated later in this chapter will help you stay brief.

Create Curiosity

Say just enough to get them curious. Give them a good nugget or two that allows them a little information about what you are doing, enough to get them curious, and then move on.

Qualify the Prospect

This business is not for everyone. The best time to find this out is during the contact. For this reason, contacting someone who is not interested is not a waste of time; it is actually a time *savings*. Showing this business to someone who is not qualified is like trying to sell a bathing suit to a polar bear. A proper contact qualifies the prospect to make sure they are at least a little ambitious and looking for something more in their financial life.

Posture

The contacting step should demonstrate your posture or belief in the business. *Posture* is your mental stance or level of conviction about what you are doing; the higher your belief in the business, the higher your posture. The more excited and enthusiastic you are, the higher your posture. Posture is communicated through your enthusiasm level, the excitement in your voice, the confidence and conviction with which you speak, and the assertiveness with which you conduct yourself. (Be careful, just because you have posture doesn't mean you shouldn't be friendly and nice. Never become pushy or "salesy.") Somehow, prospects have built-in posture detectors. They get a "feeling" about you and what you are doing. They know immediately if you believe in it. Therefore, it is important for you to have proper posture. This can be developed by immersing yourself in the training system. Listen to CD's on a regular basis, and subscribe to the "maximum" theory: don't try to discover the *minimum* amount of CD listening that will bring success, go for the *maximum*! That will be one of the fastest ways to develop belief and conviction in the business. Posture is further developed as you gain experience rotating each of the five steps in the pattern. The more you listen, attend, read, and learn, and the more you *do*, the higher your posture and the better your results.

It is possible to have too much posture, just as it is possible to have too little posture. Too much posture makes you appear pushy. Too little posture makes you appear weak and unconvinced about the business. As we sometimes say, the correct level of posture is somewhere between "wimp" on one side, and "jerk" on the other.

One important thing to do before making contacts is to put yourself in the right frame of mind. This involves reminding yourself of who you are and why you are building the business in the first place. Think about your dreams, and all the things you want to accomplish through this Team business vehicle. Then think about your dreads, and all the things you'd like to improve or change or get away from in your current situation. As a general rule, we should never get too far away from our reason why, and this is doubly true when we are making contacts. Our dreams will fuel us to take the action steps necessary to build our business.

Next, think about what a great opportunity you are offering to the people you are about to call. If it's good enough for you, it will be good enough for them, too. If it has changed your life and given you new hopes and dreams, wouldn't they awaken to the same great things if given the chance and the same information you've received? Of course! And that's the chance you are about to offer them as you make the call. Picture in your mind having a big business and accomplishing your dreams. Would you hesitate to call someone about such a great business if it had already worked for you? You have to first see it in order to achieve it. Then you have to act according to what you see. Develop the frame of mind that you are a multi-million dollar business owner and you are making contact with a potential new partner in the venture. It is as if you are calling to arrange an interview. If they are not interested, no big deal. If they are interested, great. Either way, you are going to fill the position. As you build this business, remember, you don't need any one particular person. No one is "your guy," your key to success. You can't lead anyone you *need*. That's posture, and these are just some of the ways to put yourself into the right posture when contacting.

Obtain a Written Appointment

The contact should end with an appointment written or typed into your calendar, *and* the calendar of the prospect. A loose appointment is no appointment.

Make the Appointment Soon

The appointment should not be too distant in the future. The more time between your initial contact and the appointment, the more likely a cancellation or "no show" will occur.

Make No "Confirmation Calls"

The appointment should require no "confirmation call." A booked appointment is a booked appointment. You will be there when you said you will be there. Do not allow yourself to get trapped in a situation where the prospect says to you, "Call me to confirm," or "Give me a call and we'll figure out the time." The appointment should be booked for a specific time and place, and no further phone calls or conversations are necessary. We have found that a call to confirm is an invitation for a cancellation.

Answer Questions With Questions

It is best to answer a question with a question. This is easier if you have a few response questions memorized ahead of time.

Make Appointments at the Prospect's Home

This principle is specific to one-on-ones. Always try to make the appointment at *the prospect's house*. People feel the most comfortable and hospitable in their own homes. Although their home environment may possibly be a little distracting to you (small children, dogs, etc.), it isn't distracting to *them*. Your best chance of getting the prospect to listen is if you have the appointment at their house. The worst chance for a successful meeting is if you book the appointment at their place of employment. First of all, it isn't too professional because they are there to do a job and you are potentially interfering with that responsibility. But of even bigger concern is the way people behave when they are sitting behind their own desk, playing the big shot, dictating terms to anybody who sits on the other side of it. Only slightly better are appointments at restaurants. This is because there are distractions galore, and restaurants are very easy locations for prospects *not* to go! More than once have we sat in a restaurant, sipping our water, telling the waitress to wait just a few more minutes for that person we're sure is going to arrive at any minute.

Have the Prospect's Spouse Present for the Plan

When the prospect is married, always try to have the prospect's spouse present at the appointment. This is critical because it doubles the odds of having somebody get excited about the business. Not every couple comes into the business with the same excitement level on the part of both spouses. As with all decisions (getting married, having children, etc.) usually one spouse is more interested in the idea than the other. It is only natural. Showing the plan to *both* partners at the same time increases the chance of getting at least one of them excited. Additionally, it ensures that whoever "wears the pants" in the family will see the plan, too. Time and again we have gotten one spouse excited about the business, but when they went home and tried to relate their excitement, they got shot down before they even got started. "The boss" squelched the idea in its infancy. This is because *they* don't know how to properly present the plan yet. You are the professional (or are hopefully becoming one!). *You* should be the one to explain it to all potential partners.

Contact in "Batches"

Contacting is best when done in batches. One very successful business owner once taught that when contacting, consider the word "blitz." Generally, the more contacts you do in a short amount of time, the better you will do. This is because you will be in practice and not "rusty." Sometimes we hear people say, "I've set a goal to make one contact a day." While that is a worthy goal, the likelihood is that most of those contacts will be done when the business owner is not warmed up. Making several calls or contacts in a row can develop a momentum factor that actually increases results. For that reason, clump your contacts together. Make several in the same sitting. Fill up your calendar with appointments all in one shot.

Over-Invite People for Group Meetings

This principle is specific to group meetings. Always invite more people than you want to attend. This is because not all the people who commit to attending will be able to make it. Some will have legitimate reasons for missing the appointment. Others will simply be too nice to say "no" on the phone even though they are really not interested. Invite at least twice the number of people you would actually like to have in attendance. (We will talk in more detail about conducting house plans in the next chapter.)

These are the main principles involved in contacting. Understanding them, and sticking to them, will play a big part in your success rate.

Specifics of Contacting

The specifics of contacting build on the principles. There are three specific ways people can be contacted about this business. The first is what we might call a "physical" contact. This is one in which someone is telephoned or spoken to in person (though we usually recommend the telephone). The second method of contacting someone is through exposing them to the products. The final method involves exposing them to the system.

Contacting with a Script

One of the best ways to make the initial contact is either over the phone or face to face in a quick, to-the-point conversation. A contacting script is a pre-written approach that has been proven to work. We recommend following a proven script as closely as possible. Again, we often hear people say things like, "But that will sound corny to people who know me," or "I could never say that." So they proceed to contact people using their own approach and experience poor results. Eventually, they try a proven script and are amazed at the difference. Scripts work. The words have been chosen carefully, and the entire structure has been developed through hundreds of real-life contacts. As an example the following is a script that has been proven to be very successful:

Hello (prospect name), this is (your name). Have I caught you at a bad time? (If yes, ask when would be a good time to call again. If no, continue).

The reason I'm calling is, have you ever heard of (your upline leader)? He (or she) has helped pioneer a business on the Internet and I'm working directly with him (or her). They're expanding right now and that's why I'm calling.

I can't promise anything, but I'd like to get together to discuss the details.

How's _____ night at _____ o'clock?

[If they ask a question at this point, reply by asking the following question in reply]:

Have you ever heard of the book *Leading the Consumer Rebellion*?

[Whatever their response, continue with the following]:

It will make more sense when we get together. How's _____ night at _____ o'clock?

81

[If they ask another question, reply with the next question]:

Have you ever heard of Michael Dell's "Three C's"?

[Whatever their response, continue with the following]:

It will make more sense when we get together. How's _____ night?

[If they ask yet another question, respond with your final question]:

Have you ever heard of the Robert Kiyosaki's *Cashflow Quadrant?*
(OR, as an alternative)
Do you know anything about the Sports/Nutrition Industry?

[Again, respond by trying to book the appointment.]

I've got to draw it out for you for it to make sense. Will _____ night work for you?

[Or, another effective response is]:

It's a lot like trying to give a haircut over the phone. It will make more sense when we meet in person. Will _____ night work for you?

[If you still are unable to book the appointment, the individual is probably not really open to looking at anything. Close out the contact with]:

Well (prospect name), it doesn't' sound like you're interested in looking at anything right now, why don't we forget it. If you ever change your mind, give me a call. I've got to go.

This script, or something very close to it, will work. Be very careful before making any changes to it. Get the input of your experienced, higher level up-line before making alterations. Sometimes, one or two simple word changes are all that is necessary to reduce its effectiveness. So be careful. Rehearse this script over and over by reading it aloud to yourself. Practice so that it doesn't sound "scripted." Eventually, you will get to where you can contact without even thinking about it, most likely using words of the same script over and over. But especially in the beginning, use the script. Have these words in front of you. Lay out the brochure and have it close at hand as you make your calls. The closer you stay to the words of a proven script, the higher your success rate at booking appointments.

The above script is designed primarily for inviting prospects to see the plan in a one-on-one setting. With minor modifications, this same script works well when inviting prospects to house plans. After asking, "How's _____ night at _____ o'clock?" Inform them of the location of the house plan. "Great. It's at my house. Do you remember how to get here? (if question is applicable). If the house plan is at a home other than your own, it is a good idea to offer to pick them up. Very few people feel comfortable just walking into a stranger's home. Besides, there is a much higher possibility of them actually showing up if you pick them up! These simple details can easily be arranged within the body of the above script. The key is to accomplish the major objectives of the contact, and get them to see the plan.

Contacting with Phone Call Sessions

Another specific way to contact prospective new business owners is through an event called a phone call or contacting session. At these meetings, groups of business owners get together and make a bunch of contacts all at once and record their results on a board for all to see. Friendly competitions can be arranged where the business owners break up into teams and see who can book the most appointments. There can be prizes awarded for individual and team achievement. The reason phone call sessions are so popular and work so effectively is because we are encouraged by the performance of each other. When we see our partners making calls and getting results, it inspires us to do the same. There is power in a group of like-minded individuals all running for their goals and dreams together. Contacting is well enabled by this "group inertia." Also, competition is fun and can spur us onward. Where we may hesitate to sit by ourselves and break through mental barriers, the heat of a competition, even if it's for who buys the pizza or ice cream, can push us out of our shell and compel us to act. Usually, once someone has participated in a phone call session and proven to himself that he can make contacts successfully, it is easier for him to continue making calls on his own later. This is because the phone call session helped build his belief. The people at a phone call session see the business working right before their very eyes. They see others having success. They see first-hand that the contacting scripts work. These experiences give confidence to the new business owner that he or she can *also* achieve success.

Phone call sessions can be a good way to spark a particular group of business owners into action. A leader can review his group and decide that not enough plans are being shown in a given location and sponsor a phone call session to help get things moving. This provides an excellent format for training, answering questions, associating, and building confidence. Most importantly, though, phone call sessions work. Entire organizations wouldn't exist today if someone hadn't called together a group of business owners and hosted a phone calling session to get things moving. If such an event becomes available, be sure and take advantage of it.

Contacting with Products

One of the immense benefits of our focus on the Sports/Nutrition industry is the quality and marketability of the products involved (more on this later). The XS brand of energy drinks are already the number one selling American made energy drink! They are priced extremely competitively, and quite nearly "sell themselves." The marketing around the Sports/Nutrition products is top-notch, and many of the products were wildly successful in the conventional marketplace before they became exclusive to those of us building this business. Because of these reasons, the Sports/Nutrition products themselves can be used in contacting others about the business idea.

Here's the concept. What is one of the most natural, expected things to ask someone after they've stepped into your home? Offer them something to drink! We all do it! It's a major custom of our society. Failure to offer someone a drink is even considered rude! For how long have we been offering people products produced by a company with which we have no contract? Products for which we can make no income, products that we even had to pay for ourselves!? In effect, what we were doing was advertising for someone else for free! Now, when you have a contract with one of the hottest selling energy drinks in the country, you can offer your *own* product! This can be done on your lunchbreak at work, at the playground with other parents, during your shared commutes to work, on camping trips, wherever it is customary to whip out a refreshment! The possibilities are endless. And each one of these possibilities will be a chance for a contact about your business. When someone sees you drinking an XS energy drink, or when you hand them one to drink, the natural question is, "What is this?" or "Where did you get this?" Either question leads to the ability to tell someone about your business. "It's from my Internet business," you might say. "It's the number one selling American made energy drink, and you can only get them from Internet business owner's like myself," one could reply. This naturally leads to more questions about *the business behind the product*. However, it is best to avoid too much "on the spot" explaining about the business. Just as we said before, it is much more effective to use the *contact* as a way to set up an appointment where the plan can be presented later. This is true for these face-to-face situations, as well. Once the person indicates an interest by asking questions, simply give one of the two following responses (whichever is most applicable): "It's not really appropriate to get into it here (if you are at work, or on someone else's time, for instance) but I'd be happy to call you about it later," or, "I don't really have enough time to get into it right now, but I could call you later." Or, "Pretty good, isn't it? How would you like to be on the profit side of the number one selling American made energy drink on the market?" Using any of these, you've opened the door of curiosity and gotten a phone number to make a contact according to the guidelines taught earlier in this chapter.

By using products to initiate contacts, you are also demonstrating a very easy method of building your business that the new people joining your team will remember and easily be able to duplicate. That is why there are sample products associated with getting started in the business. In effect, these products become the business owner's "advertising." And each new person that gets started can immediately be armed with products to use in contacting people. For this reason, make sure you always have some products on you to consume and some to hand out to others. You are literally turning every occasion of refreshing yourself into a possible new business contact! You are going to eat and drink *anyway*, why not get something out of it?

Contacting with the System

Perhaps the least common, but still an effective method of contacting people, is by exposing them to the exciting training materials from the Team's system. This might occur if someone has the opportunity to listen to a CD or browse through one of the books from the system. "What's this?" they usually ask, to which the business owner can then respond according to the principles we discussed and book an appointment or show the plan right then and there. There are many stories about people who got into the business because the driver of the car in which they were car pooling was listening to CD's from the Team, or perhaps they saw one of the Team DVD's playing in someone's living room. Remember,

86

truth is sweet to the ears. If someone is looking for a better life financially, and they get exposed to the truths in our system, they will be interested in learning more.

Summary

Making a list of names, then contacting those names to book appointments, are very important steps to building your business. Without becoming adept at both of these steps, it will be very difficult to build a strong and profitable business. Take the time to develop proficiency. Become a professional. Update your names list all the time, and make contacts to book appointments on a regular basis. At first, your up-line support team will help you. Eventually, though, you need to take over the helm of the ship. After all, it's your business. The sooner you master these first two steps, the sooner you'll be ready to move on to the next three, which begin with the most important of all, "showing the plan."

Personal Stories

Names: Chuck and Nancy Cullen
Former Occupations: High School English Teacher,
Basketball and Track Coach; Kindergarden Teacher

When I was first introduced to the Team, I had explored every other income generation idea I could come up with! I tried everything from rental properties to speculative build real estate transactions to selling stuff on eBay! My wife, Nancy, was always less than enthused with my next "big idea." Everything I tried worked to a degree, but it was always a one time influx of money, and then I was on to the next thing. I could not figure out how to get a steady stream of income flowing outside of my job. I always knew there had to be a better way. I had taken the conventional "get your degree" advice. In fact, between Nancy and me, we had four of them including Master's degrees! No matter what I tried, I was not getting ahead financially. Part of the problem was a lack of financial discipline, but the majority of the problem was a serious "thinking" problem. I was weighed down with conventional employee or self-employed thinking. The questions I would ask myself were things like "how can I get a better job", or, "what type of business can I create and operate?"

After working as a high school English teacher for five years, I decided that I couldn't create the lifestyle I desired with a teacher's income. The only other option, or so I thought at the time, was to venture out into the world of self-employment. I teamed up with my brother in a manufacturer's representative business and quickly learned the laws of the jungle. As a self-employed business owner, it was truly feast-or-famine income. I was constantly in pursuit of the next sale, and I could not see an end in sight. There was no way I could put away enough money to ever retire. I soon began to lose all hope.

When I was introduced to this business, I was three years into self-employment and ready to make some changes in both my personal and professional life. Nancy and I had our first child on the way, and I was ready to do anything I could to make sure my growing family would be financially secure. I saw the Team as my only hope. I immediately set the goal to replace my income as fast as I could, so I could spend time with our new baby.

I think when I got started on the Team, I did everything wrong that I could possibly do wrong! In fact, the only thing that I did *right* was get started! A group of us that had just joined the Team together decided we knew more than Orrin and Chris (the authors of this book) and the leaders of the system. We held our own meetings (in a bar!), made recordings of our talks (with all our own financial wisdom on them) and were going to show the world that we could do this idea better than the Team could! It was funny, really, to think that the idea of the Team gave us hope, but we decided to follow our own ideas instead! What we didn't yet realize was that success begins with information from the correct source. The best experience is *somebody else's* experience. The shortest way across a mine field is in the footsteps of someone who has safely made it across. But for a while, we were happy to plow our own trail. The results, as you would expect, weren't that impressive. That's when our mentor's patience in us really paid off. He was there to gently lead us into the Team system when we were ready. As the saying goes, "When the student is ready, the teacher will appear."

I knew one thing for sure: I was going to make this business work, no matter what! So I eventually learned to work with a mentor that already had financial results through the business. That made all the difference. After eighteen months of hard work and the support of a mentor (and the use of the Team system which actually worked), Nancy and I were able to build our business to the point that we could both be stay-at-home parents. Most of the hard work simply involved staying disciplined enough to change our thinking, and becoming humble enough to listen to someone with results.

Everything in our life has changed. We are now stress-free, debt-free, and job-free. We give all the credit to God. We understand where all our blessings, including the blessing of this great business, come from.

Names: Joe and Jane McGuire
Former Occupations: Podiatrist; Retail Store Owner

When I first saw the business plan, I was probably living the typical, new doctor's life for "these days." I had been in private, solo practice for two-and-a-half years and had built up three offices. The work schedule was full, while trying to raise three children. My wife, Jane, and I had practiced delayed gratification for eleven years of school: eating Ramen noodles and driving junk cars. The debt-load for most new doctors is staggering, to say the least. While I was in school and looking forward to a rewarding career, the debts grew higher and higher.

As it turned out, Medicare and insurance companies had a different plan for me and my family. They cut reimbursements to "Health Care Providers" (doctors) across the board and our income plummeted. I was definitely looking for something. But not *this* business. My initial feeling upon seeing the plan was not one of excitement or skepticism. I just thought, "For the cost of a new Five Iron (the approximate price to get started), I have nothing to lose. That business probably works for some people, but probably not for me. But hey, you never know. Maybe someday." Well, that someday came shortly after that.

After another round of reimbursement cuts, I finally went to a Team Open Meeting and realized that this business *could work* for me because it had a *system* I could learn from. *And* this system would help me build my business. I was excited that I wouldn't need buildings, employees, massive inventory, bank loans, lines of credit or anything else that would give me ulcers.

The education we've gotten through the Team system has been incredible. We've learned how to leverage time. We've gained our freedom, and no longer depend upon insurance companies and government bureaus for income. To this day I haven't figured out why I ever chose a career path (the medical profession) where I would have to depend on people who made decisions that weren't in my best interest. By far, the thing that I love best about the Team is the Win-Win principle. It is the best of the best of what free market economics represents.

Life has changed. Here is a partial list of things that can happen to you, like they have happened for Jane & me: Being "job optional," wake up everyday when done sleeping, more time with family, no financial stress, eliminate debt, more money at the end of the month than days left in the month, more friends and deeper relationships with friends, more travel, able to take care of family members and give more to church and charity, receive the best business mentorship, establish better relationships within our family, help others through the Team system, become more involved in faith and church, and go to every one of the kids' football and basketball games (even if they occur during the day and during the week).

Building the Team business is the best decision I have ever made, outside the one I made to marry my lovely wife, Jane. Until you're free, you just don't know how great life can be!

"Success lies in forming the habit of doing things that failures
don't like to do."
- Albert Gray

"Only do what only you can do."
- unknown

"Never judge a person's horsepower by his exhaust."
- unknown

"Opportunity is missed by most people because it is dressed in
overalls and looks like work."
- Thomas Edison

"Don't wait for your ship to come in, swim out to it."
- unknown

Name: COOL-GUY CARL

Quote: "My man, I had nine different ways
to become a millionaire already.
Besides, I am way too cool to do
something like that!"

Chapter 6

Activity, Part Two
Showing the Plan

After Making a List and Contacting, the remaining steps in the Five Step Pattern are:

3. Showing the plan
4. Following through
5. Rotating the pattern – getting them started

If the purpose of the contact is to book an appointment, then the purpose of the appointment is to "show the plan." This is where the rubber meets the road. Showing the plan is the most constructive part of building your business. As far as we can tell, people who don't get the plan shown to them don't get in the business! Therefore, to build your business bigger, you will need to show the plan! This chapter will deal exclusively with that step of the process.

House Plans and One-on-Ones

There are generally two types of plans to be shown, as we covered only slightly in the last chapter. A *one-on-one* is when an individual or couple presents the plan to another individual or couple. The second type of plan is called a *house plan*. This is where several people are invited to someone's home to see the plan in a group setting.

House Plans

House plans (also called group meetings in this book) are by far the most efficient way to share the Team business with prospective business owners. This is because house plans require just one plan to be shown, but several people get to see it at once. For this reason, house plans are the plan of choice. To build a team fast, house plans must be a regular occurrence in the team builder's calendar. To build the business without an avid use of house plans is to paddle a canoe with a serving spoon (or perhaps even a tea spoon).

There are many ways to make a house plan effective. First of all, the newest, most excited, *deepest* (furthest down the line of sponsorship in an organization) business owner should be the one to host such an event. The leading business builder should make sure that this host couple or individual is properly assisted in building a names list, and in contacting *more than enough prospects* from that list. Next, the leader can invite other business owners who are up-line of the host couple to "plug into" that house plan. Possibly, this invitation can be conditional; for example: only the business owners who can also bring new prospects to the house plan are invited. Finally, the leader can then plug in some individuals from his or her other organizations to come along with him or her. This will demonstrate how a proper house plan should run, and give them a chance to build their belief, gain some time around an excited group of people, and to build a better relationship with the leader (in this example, the one showing the plan). This may be a bit too involved to delve into further here, but remember, once you get to that point, to make house plans the cornerstone of your business, and to pack everything into them that you can to make them as effective as possible in building your business.

One-on-Ones

One-on-Ones are the filler in a business builder's calendar. They are used when it is temporarily not possible to set up an effective house plan in an area, or when it simply works out to show a certain individual the plan. One-on-Ones should not be avoided, however, but rather they should be used to develop a cluster of people, both business owners and interested parties, that can then participate in an upcoming house plan that brings it all together. One-on-Ones support an upcoming house plan.

House plans and one-on-one plans are slightly different in their set-up and conduct. Each will be addressed individually in the discussions to follow. As in the previous chapter, we will talk about *principles* of showing the plan first and *specifics* second.

Principles of Showing the Plan

There are several resources that can assist you in learning the principles of showing the plan. Of course, the aforementioned *How to Get Started* materials are a great place to begin. A further perspective on showing the plan can be gained by listening to audio recordings dealing specifically with that subject. What you will discover is that there are five main purposes of showing the plan:

1. Make a Friend
2. Find a Need
3. Transfer the Feeling
4. Involve Them in the System
5. Book a Follow-Through

Make a Friend

This entire business is built on relationships. That is why there is so much emphasis in the Team training system on people skills and personal growth. If one isn't relatable and likeable, there will be no basis for starting a new relationship and therefore very little chance to grow a business.

The first objective in showing the plan is to make a friend out of the prospect. This is not a technique or trick, it must be done sincerely and on a real, personal level. It begins by listening: one of life's most important, but also rarest, skills. It should be a major objective of the business owner to ask questions and get to know the prospect. Looking around the prospects' home as you prepare to show them the plan also reveals immense clues about who they are and what activities they pursue. Are there trophies on the mantle? Is there a snowmobile trailer out in the driveway? Is their home decorated with photos of children and/or grandchildren? The point is to be attentive. Pay attention to the other person. Ask and listen and learn. The objective is to get to know them. Make a friend.

There is an old phrase is the sales world that states, "You cannot sell John Brown what John Brown buys until you can see the world through John Brown's eyes." That's a little of what is happening here. The plan is to be tailored to the individual to which it is being shown. To do that properly, one must understand a little about the person on the receiving end.

Further, for a friendship to begin, the prospect must also come to like you. Relatability is the quality that endears you to others and helps you make a good first impression. The prospect should feel at ease with you and should feel that you are "real." Remember, nobody will enter into a business arrangement with someone they don't know, like, and trust. Relatability is the ability to arrive at these three qualities in the eyes of the prospect.

Unless the first objective of "making a friend" is reached, it is not only futile, but *impossible*, to move on to the second objective. So the first part of showing the plan is to make a friend out of the prospect. This must happen. If it *doesn't*, the rest of the steps either won't take place or will likely be in vain.

Find a Need

The second objective of showing the plan is to find out what the prospect wants. This is usually called a dream. What we have found, as discussed earlier, is that people often have extensive lists of "wants" or fantasies that they say they want but for which they are not willing to work. What must be done at this step is to identify the true desires of the prospect's heart. What does he or she *really* want? A dream is something that the person *needs* to have fulfilled in their life. That's why we say at this step to find a *need*. What condition, helped by money and time and more personal freedom, does the prospect long for in his or her life that won't come true without the business? What would that person do if he struck it big in his local lottery? What is the true motivation of her heart?

This may sound harder to find than it actually is. Most people are dreamers. Most people have deep yearnings for more time with their family, alleviation of debt, more security in their financial future, more friends and social opportunities, more relationships— all the types of results that the Team business can provide! This is why it is so important in the above step to make a connection with the person, because as you get to know them you will come to understand what motivates them. It will be easier to identify what rewards would make the business worth it for them.

Often we'll hear people say, "I just couldn't get a dream out of them," or "They really didn't seem to want anything." These might very well be true. But more often, the reason a prospect is closed-lipped about his or her dreams is because the business owner hasn't taken the time to initiate a relationship. If the prospects don't know, like, and trust you, they will not open up with you about their dreams and desires. Period. Also, as Diamond Lady, Amy Marks, says, "Discovering someone's dream is hard if we don't have one of our own!" Make sure *your* dreams are alive and vibrant, and that will help others open up about *their* dreams.

Remember, nobody joins this business if someone doesn't help them identify what's in it for them. Help them find their reason why, and you will help them find their way to it.

What's in it for them?

What's in it for them?

What's in it for them?

Never get more than a couple of seconds away from that question!

Transfer the Feeling

After connecting with the prospect and initiating a relationship, and after identifying what the person is looking for more of in life, it is next important to transfer a feeling of excitement and belief. Even if the prospect likes you, and even if they have legitimate goals and dreams they are willing to work to achieve, if you bore them to tears they probably won't want to become your business partner.

We cannot overemphasize the importance of enthusiasm. When contacting, showing the plan, in fact, during every step of the Five Step Pattern, it is vitally important to be enthusiastic and excited. If this is the best business opportunity that exists, if this is going to wipe out debt and allow early retirement and provide freedom and financial stability and all the dreams and goals we talk about, then it makes sense that we should be commensurably excited about it. Our enthusiasm has to match our message. Granted, if we were showing up to explain that we can help them make $3.50 a month, enthusiasm would be a little out of place. But, obviously, we are offering so much more than that. Our excitement should communicate that all by itself.

Some personalities have no problem with this. They're the type to be cracking jokes at funerals. Other personalities think they are being exciting and showing enthusiasm but everybody around them for three city blocks is falling asleep. It is important to know yourself and to which category you belong. Those whose enthusiasm is "over the top" *may* need to tone it down a bit and focus on being relate-able. Those that are even *slightly* unenthusiastic must work to increase the level of excitement demonstrated. Don't underestimate the importance of this step. Attitudes and emotions are contagious. So if you're transferring a feeling, make sure it's positive! If you're excited, be sure to notify your face!

Involve Them in the System

"The System" refers to the complete line of training aids (called "tools") and meetings provided by the Team. Properly utilized, these are to be leveraged to increase your relatability and appeal.

It may be that you are a very relatable person. You are doing a great job of connecting to the prospect, and you have identified a real need that the business can help him or her fulfill. But you still need to bring out the heavy artillery. You still need to leverage the training system to work on your behalf. There are many reasons for this.

First, excitement has a shelf life. Even if you did everything right when contacting and showing the plan, there is still the tendency of the prospect to "cool off" after you have gone. Leaving behind and promoting the correct materials, such as CD's, pamphlets, and the "first-night book," and getting them to an Open Meeting, will not only maintain the prospect's excitement level, but will also *increase* it.

Second, you will only "click" with a small percentage of the people out there. We are all different. We all have our particular temperaments and interests. These variations make it likely that we'll bond quite naturally with some people while having to work much harder at it with others. This is where the training system steps in. On each of the CD's, in the books, and at the meetings, different personalities, backgrounds, ethnicities, religious beliefs, and interests will all be represented. Even if the prospect doesn't exactly relate to you, he or she certainly will find someone within the training system with whom he or she can relate. In this way, the system broadens your relatability and therefore your effectiveness.

Third, you can't possibly be everywhere at once, meeting the needs of an increasingly larger and larger organization and answering every question or need that arises. If you start people into the system as their source of answers right up front, you will create the proper habits on their part for finding the answers to their questions. They will seek the system as their teacher and not you. This frees up enormous amounts of your time and also establishes a duplicatable pattern that they can in turn follow. Duplication, after all, is the secret to the explosive growth potential of the concept of franchising. "What do I do next?" they might ask. "Exactly what I've done with you," is the answer. "What tools do I leave them after I show them the plan?" they ask. "The same ones I left for you." See how duplication works? Utilize the system from the very beginning to bring people into the business and you are already teaching them how to get started building their own business properly.

Book a Follow Through

The fifth and final checkpoint to showing the plan is to book a "follow-through." A follow-through is the next meeting at which the business owner will get back together with the prospect and continue the process. We will explain more of how to conduct a follow-through later, but at this stage of showing the plan, it is critical that a solid time to get back together has been agreed upon by both parties, and written down.

Many, many times, ourselves included, business owners have done every step of the pattern correctly until this one. They make a great list. They do an excellent job of contacting and booking the appointment. They show an inspired, informed plan. But for some reason, at the end of the plan, they walk away without booking a solid time to get back together and continue the process. Don't make this fatal mistake. Don't leave the scene of the plan and say, "I'll call you." You might as well cross their name off the list right then and there – they will not get involved in the business. Most likely, you'll try to call them a couple of times and may or may not get in touch with them, either way, you have lost posture, and now you are "chasing" them. This represents a loss of posture and the process is over. To avoid all of this, simply book an appointment before leaving the plan!

It even helps to let the prospect know during the plan what the process will be. Tell him or her that today (the showing of the

102

plan) is only the initial meeting. At the end of the plan, you will be booking a time to get back together with them to help them further assess their potential in this business. When the prospective business owner knows what to expect, he or she is more likely to follow along.

Specifics of Showing the Plan

Understanding these general principles of showing the plan, it is now appropriate to paint in the details.

Dress

Showing up to present the business plan to someone is a chance to make a good first impression. So dress appropriately. Be a professional. For men, that means wearing a suit; the most effective of which is dark blue with a white shirt (long sleeve) and red or burgundy silk tie. For women, it means a skirt or dress. These are simple guidelines, but very effective.

Deviation from this standard has incredible ramifications. First, the crazier the colors or styles of a man's suit, the less he relates to others. This has an enormous impact on sponsoring. For women, the more revealing or intimidating their appearance, the less they will be able to relate to other women, and the more they will distract other men. Secondly, the more "off track" someone is in appearance, the more it will be duplicated by his or her organization. It doesn't take much iteration before someone shows up in a bathing suit to show the plan. (You think we're kidding!) The point is this: whether male or female, your dress should be for *business*. This means that it doesn't draw attention to itself. Your clothing should be such that *it* isn't noticed; *you* and *what you have to present* are noticed instead. The resulting impression is one of friendly professionalism that doesn't intimidate.

103

Hygiene

We hate having to even discuss this, but next is the topic of proper hygiene. It should go without saying that one should show up to represent a business looking and acting the part of a business owner. This means proper appearance in personal grooming, as well as the considerations of dress just discussed.

What do we mean? A business owner should be showered, smelling good (but not overpowering), with teeth brushed, and wearing clean, pressed clothes. Hair should be neat and not the object of distraction or conversation. Fingernails should be clean and cut short; visible piercings and corresponding jewelry should be minimized. Men should make sure they don't have yellowed collars, wrinkled suit coats, or frayed cuffs, and that their nose and ear hair is trimmed (we're serious). Facial hair has also historically been considered a possible distraction. Women should, well, women should ask their up-line women leaders what they should do. (You didn't think we were stupid enough to say something here that would risk offending the entire female gender, did you? We may have been born at night, but it wasn't *last* night!) Seriously now, our wives think women should be dressed professionally, preferably in a skirt that is longer than knee-length. Conservative fit and style will avoid distracting anyone from the main message. Remember, all of this is intended to simply allow the business and your attitude as a professional business owner to shine through, rather than your appearance. We want people to remember the possibilities the business provides in their lives, not odd features of our personal appearance, dress, or grooming (or lack thereof).

This is all just common sense. And we are certain that you, the reader, already knew all of this stuff, so you certainly wouldn't get insulted by our mentioning a few of these recommendations. After all, they will help the people on your team who *might* need to hear them. As for the people to which some of these things might apply: we, the humble authors, can't possibly know who is reading these words right now. We aren't even around! So there is no reason to take offense, we don't even know it's you this instruction was meant for! (Whew! This is tough!)

First Impressions

Another very important thing to consider when arriving to show the plan, whether to an individual, couple, or house full of people, is to be conscious of your first impression. The old saying, "You'll never get a second chance to make a good first impression," rings true.

Here are some specifics that we hope will be helpful.

First, lead with a smile. You'd be surprised what barriers can be broken down with a simple, sincere, confident smile. A smile lets the other person know you are at ease, confident, and open to them. Practice smiling before you ever say a word to someone. Practice smiling the moment someone looks at you. These things will take practice, but you will notice enormous results by the simple art of smiling. Dale Carnegie, perhaps the most famous teacher ever of people skills, ranks smiling at the top of the list of importance in human relations. The same certainly applies to the Team business. So lead with a smile in everything you do.

Second, make eye contact. It has been said that the eyes are the window to the soul. Looking at the person's eyes lets him know you are fully engaged and focused on him and what he is saying. It also gives you a great chance to "read" the other person and pick up on any non-verbal clues that will help you connect with him.

Third, learn to make a good hand shake. Don't be a "dead fish" (limp and light), and don't be a vise (bone crusher), but somewhere in-between. Also, avoid pumping the hand up and down repeatedly. We are making friends, not pumping water from a well! Stay away from pulling others into you when shaking hands, and letting go too early or too late. Remember, this is a business. Hand shaking will be common in almost every interaction here, and your handshake is a chance to show that you are a professional.

Fourth, beware of over-talking, interrupting, close-talking, and any other irritating talking maladies of which you may be guilty. We have all had to work on these from time to time, and it is a good idea to keep ourselves aware of the best conduct for endearing others to ourselves. Our favorite Tim Marks quote that should be helpful in this category is, "Just because it happened to you, doesn't make it interesting!" (Ouch!)

This whole category of first impressions will be addressed repeatedly in the books on people skills available in the training system. It is safe to say that no matter how adept in dealing with people that we become, and no matter how high we rise in the business financially, it is never time to relax on the basic principles of getting along with people. We should all read about the great principles and specifics of people skills on a regular basis.

Environment

For One-on-One Plans

We discussed in the chapter on contacting how important it is to try to schedule the appointment for a one-on-one at the prospect's home. Assuming this has been accomplished, there are a couple of important related details.

Show up on time. Tardiness is a sign of a lack of discipline, disrespect for the other person, or both. Be prompt. Please note, though, that this does not mean be early. You don't want to appear eager or as if you have nothing better to do than to visit them that evening.

Enter someone else's home with respect, and never forget that you are a guest. Greet them at the door with a handshake, and as you enter, notice if they would like you to remove your shoes, etc. Introduce your spouse, and get an introduction to their spouse. Remember, small courtesies go a long way toward making friends. Pet their dog. Say hello to any children that come around. Be interested in their family. When you pull up to their home, don't take the obvious parking spot of the owner or box them in.

Next, direct the meeting to take place at their kitchen table. Don't let them set you down on couches or quarantine you to some formal living room. Simply say, "You know what? I'm going to probably want to draw some things out. Would you mind if we used your kitchen table?"

Most people are very cordial and hospitable. They will likely offer you a drink or something. The general rule is to always accept. It allows them to serve you a little and makes them feel a bit more at ease.

Don't get distracted or annoyed at interruptions. The patience you show with their household is a sign of respect that they will appreciate.

For House Plans

While learning how to show the plan, new business owners usually give their business the fastest start by hosting a house plan - where their up-line comes to their home to show the plan to friends and family.

Let's consider the arrangement of the room. The board and easel should be placed at the opposite end of the room from where people enter. This minimizes distractions. For the same reason, children should be out of the room and with baby-sitters, preferably at a different location. Pets should be tucked away in another room where they can't get into the crowd of people and cause distraction. The best plan presenter in the world cannot compete with a cute child or friendly pet.

The homeowner or host of the house plan should be very careful regarding his or her conduct. It has the biggest impact on the attitude and interest level of prospective business owners. For instance, as the time to begin the presentation draws near, the host should never say things like, "I expected more people than this," or "I can't believe John isn't here," or "They said they would be here." These seemingly harmless little statements kill the interest of the prospects that are on hand to see the business. It makes them wonder what's wrong with *them*. For the same reason, the host should not set out too many chairs in advance. It is much better to bring chairs out as people arrive than to have a bunch of empty chairs sitting there when the plan begins. In general, the host should be excited, friendly, and professional.

The business owner showing the plan should arrive at exactly ten minutes after the starting time. This is because the main speaker doesn't want to be forced into "small talk" with prospects before sharing the plan, because it diminishes posture. (The homeowner should be informed of this in advance, so he or she isn't concerned when presenter is ten minutes late.) Ideally, when the presenter arrives, he or she should be greeted by the host of the meeting (usually the homeowner) who will help carry the board and easel inside and set it up. Immediately, the host should then introduce the presenter in front of the crowd. A proper introduction should focus on the plan presenter, *not* the business itself. The host should describe the accomplishments of the presenter in verbage that the audience can understand and relate to, the purpose being to create a desire on the part of each of the prospects to listen to what the presenter has to share. The feeling of the crowd ought to be, "Wow. I can't wait to hear what this person has to say!"

Perhaps an example is in order. A proper introduction of a house plan speaker should go something like this: "Hello everybody. I have the honor tonight to introduce our speaker. This gentleman has his master's degree in engineering, was a senior engineer in the auto industry, and then got involved in what he's going to show you tonight. He has an enormous business, has been recognized for hitting some of the highest levels in this business, his wife was able to leave her job because of the income they now make through this business, and we've got him here tonight! He has spoken on stages in front of thousands of people, and he is in demand all over the country. We are very glad he could make it here to our house tonight. Please help me welcome, Mr. _____." Often the person being introduced doesn't have the long list of credentials like the person in this example. In that case, it is still important to edify the person, not the business by making truthful statements like, "He is wise beyond his years," or "His entrepreneurial spirit was evident when he started his own lawn-mowing business at the age of 16. He is an incredible student of self-help books and is learning directly from some of this nation's most successful business owners. I'm excited to be learning from him tonight." Obviously the introduction should be changed to fit the exact qualifications of the speaker, but these examples should serve as a guide. Remember to introduce the *speaker* and not the *business.*

Refreshments should be kept simple, and should generally be served after the presentation. The purpose of having refreshments is to provide a good way to "break up" the meeting at the end, to avoid chaotic group question-and-answer sessions, and to demonstrate the great Sports/Nutrition products we represent. The host or hostess should be prepared to have samples of many of the energy drink flavors and meal-replacement and protein bars on hand. The speakers should bring some of their own just to be sure. This is one of the most important reasons to always have an ample supply of sample products in stock at all times. Product samples provide a tangible, credible demonstration of the business. Prospects like something at the end of the presentation that they can "sink their teeth into." Our Sports/Nutrition line literally fills that need. For more information on what to do during the refreshments time, please see the section on "After the Plan" at the end of this chapter. Specifics on how a host closes a meeting may be found there as well.

Content

Now that we've discussed how to set the correct environment, it's time to consider the content of the plan itself. Assuming you will be showing the plan, "you" or imperative sentences in this chapter will be referring to the person showing the plan. Remember, though, that the content of the plan isn't nearly as important as your attitude, enthusiasm, and posture during the plan. Some people get hung up on teaching all the details or hitting every segment of the plan just right. It is not the plan that counts; it's the connection to the prospect. The most successful plan presenters are not the ones who get every detail right and hit all the points. The most successful are the ones who connect the best with people and demonstrate relevancy to the prospect's dreams.

For *One-on-Ones in particular:* Once getting seated at the kitchen table, as described above, initiate the process with some questions to get to know the prospect. Ask them about their family. Ask them about anything you spotted in their home that sug-

109

gests their interests and hobbies. Ask them about their profession. A good acronym that may be of help here is "F.O.R.M.", which stands for Family, Occupation, Recreation, and Message. The first three are great areas to cover before arriving at the "message" you want to share. If the prospect is a good friend or family member, obviously this part of the process is unnecessary (but it would be funny to try!) Also, this step is not really possible at house plans.

The purpose of this conversation, doing a one-on-one is for you to find out about the prospect. What are his or her strengths? What have they already accomplished in life? What is their world-view? Specifically, what things about them can you find out that allow you to be able to believe in there success? This is not some cryptic technique, but a sincere attempt to get to know the prospect. You must find out some things about them so you can show them why the business will work for them. This is also where you might gain some insight into their dreams and aspirations.

Because of all this conversation, it will not and should not be possible to "show" the whole plan. Once you have effectively bonded with the prospect and gotten to know them, the "plan" simply consists of hitting some of the high points of the opportunity. You want them to have a reason to delve into the materials you leave them and attend an upcoming Open Meeting, anyway.

The major points to cover in the plan, particularly house plans, are:
1. Three Intersecting Trends
2. ESBI
3. 45 Year Plan
4. Three C's
5. Distribution Boxes
6. Franchising and Duplication
7. Pyramids vs. Team Building

Three Intersecting Trends

Begin the plan by drawing out the three intersecting trends, which are the Internet, franchising, and distribution. Take a brief moment to highlight how the Team is in a unique position to

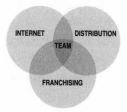

capitalize on these three hot trends. This is a great introduction
for our business and where it is positioned. This also gives you
something to which you can refer throughout the plan. The purpose of this step is to help the prospective business partner understand we are in the right place, doing the right thing, at the right
time.

ESBI

Next, draw out and explain Robert Kiyosaki's *Cash Flow
Quadrant*, featuring ESBI. The "E" stands for Employee. The "S"
stands for Self-Employed. The "B" represents a "B-Type" business,
and the "I" refers to "Investors." According to Kiyosaki, these represent the four main ways to make money.

Briefly explain each of the categories. Show how on the left side
of the quadrant 95% of the people are fighting over 5% of the
money, whereas on the right side of the quadrant it is exactly the
opposite. Relate your own story at this point; assuming you started your financial life somewhere on the left side of the quadrant
like the rest of us. Tell them about how you felt stuck in a rut (if
you did, of course), or whatever it was about your pre-Team exis-
tence that made you decide to get involved with this business. The
point here is to help the prospect understand that he or she is *not*

doing "pretty good." This part of the plan should help people break out of their comas of complacency. NOTE: It is important that you use your own situation on the left side of the quadrant to show the downside of living on that side and earning money in those ways. **Never use the prospect or his or her occupation as a negative example. The general principle is: you put all bad stuff on yourself; you put all good stuff on them.** "Bob," you might say, "you're probably doing pretty well in your job as a dentist (or whatever Bob does), but as for me, I couldn't stand going into my engineering job day after day, knowing how much I would make in a year before the year even began," etc. In this way, you help relate the futility of the left side of the quadrant without insulting the prospect or what he or she does.

This is also the section of the plan in which you relate the difference between trading time for money on a job or self-employed situation (E and S), and developing ongoing, residual income by investing time into something that brings a long-term return, such as Investing or a B-Type business (I and B). It will be helpful to draw out the example of a village needing a fresh water supply. The two methods of providing the water are through bucket carrying (the left side of the quadrant, E and S), and through construction of a pipeline (the right side of the quadrant, B and I). For a clearer reference to these concepts, get a copy of the books: *The Cashflow Quadrant*, *The Parable of the Pipeline*, and *Leading the Consumer Rebellion* from your up-line.

It is a good idea to sprinkle "the dream" throughout this section of the plan. If we are talking about developing residual income and freeing up our time, it is a likely spot for you to ask the prospect what they would do with extra time or a background residual income. This sort of thing can be done throughout the entire plan, of course, but this section is particularly effective.

Remember, the whole purpose of explaining the Cashflow Quadrant is to help the prospect understand that he or she probably has needs either in the time department, or with respect to income. Most people, if honest, would admit to a need for more of both!

45 Year Plan

The "45 Year Plan" demonstrates support for the life Kiyosaki claims the people on the left side of the Cashflow Quadrant experience. Again, you can use this diagram to show the financial life you were living before the Team business came along. The 45 Year Plan is a graph taken from originally government-published data that shows that the average citizen is going to work most of their

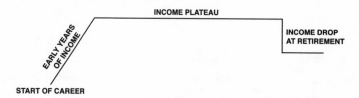

life at an income plateau, and then experience a massive fall-off in their income at retirement. This graph is particularly helpful because most people are under the illusion that "somehow" things will get better if they just keep at it. The diagram *clearly* shows that *not* to be the case for 95% of the people. Also, people tend to spend a lot more time planning their next vacation than they do their financial futures, and showing this graph gets them thinking long term.

Perhaps the biggest thing to understand about the 45 year plan is *not only* does it takes 45 years to complete, *but* even at the end of 45 years, (except in very, very rare cases), one still doesn't get to live the life of one's dreams! The time is gone. The dreams never showed up.

Three C's

At this point of the plan, the presenter begins discussing the three intersecting trends he or she drew out in the beginning. The first of these trends is the Internet.

Michael Dell, billionaire founder of Dell Computer Corporation, shared some information at a symposium in Detroit several years ago. Some of the Team's leaders were on hand at that event, and they learned a great way to explain the position of our business relative to the Internet. We have taken to calling the concept Dell shared that day, "The Three C's."

To explain the Three C's, draw out the following diagram for the prospect:

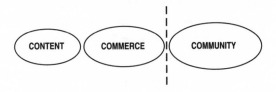

The Three C's are Content, Commerce, and Community, in increasing order of importance.

The first "C", *Content* describes the fact that business today is best conducted online, on the Internet, where the trends are the biggest any of us will see in our life times. The Internet and electronic commerce are not even considered to be just big trends anymore. The Internet is said by many to be the dawn of a new *age*. The Industrial Age is dead and the Information Age is upon us. The good news is that the Team is positioned exactly in the right place to take advantage of these facts. Business owners affiliated with the Team have access to enormous content: over 1200 companies and many of their products, over 100 complete websites, and over 1 million individual stock keeping units. That's a huge amount of content to have online! It is important to narrow the product focus down at this point. While the Team has access to an enormous selection of products and services, be sure and explain how the Team's strategy is to focus in on the most effective products offered. These are the Sports/Nutrition products. The reason for this is that the "wellness" industry is one of the fastest growing consumer markets today. The Team's products are leaders in their field and were in enormous demand under a conventional "store sales" approach (before they became exclusively sold online), and they are the most properly priced, financially compensated products that we have available. Tell the prospects that they will have an opportunity to sample some of these products after the presentation.

The next "C" is *Commerce.* The point with this "C" is that it is not enough to have a website; any idiot can build a website, and many actually have. (If you don't believe us, we'll provide a few web addresses for you as proof!) There must be "bricks and mortar" to go along with the "clicks and orders" of the website. This is where orders are processed and money changes hands. The Team has this "C" covered as well. We have "no questions asked" guarantee policies in place, and the shipping accuracy is world-class. There are also 1-800 phone numbers to dial where customers can actually talk to *humans* and not a machine! So without proper Commerce capability, having Content online doesn't amount to much, but the Team is plugged into both Content *and* Commerce capability, which brings us to the final and most important "C".

Community is the idea that we as humans are habit-forming creatures. We get into routines that are predictable and useful for marketers in determining what we buy, where we buy, and why. Brand loyalty, shopping patterns, and spending habits are all useful pieces of information in the hands of product marketers. The point Dell made that afternoon about the importance of Community was that developing a community of loyal buyers, who will come into your store again and again, is the key to developing a strong commerce business. Basically, most retail businesses are established in this manner. But accomplishing that same type of habitual loyalty *online* is much more difficult. If and when a company figured out how to do that, they would dominate online commerce. That's where the Team comes in. We specialize in that very thing. For the most part, we contract with others to provide the world-class Content and Commerce capability that we need. **It's the building of Communities that is our *core competency.* It's what we are the best at. In effect, Dell had told us that day (without even knowing it), that if we could do what we were already doing, we would have an explosive business! We already knew we were growing fast, now we had a billionaire's explanation as to why!** This is the main point the plan presenter is trying to make by relating this whole Three C's section.

When explaining this concept of building communities, it

should be expanded to bring the **dream** back into view for the prospect. Remember, all the great logic in the world is not nearly as important to a prospect as "What's in it for them?"! So draw the community circle as a "Want Circle," and compare it to a much smaller "Actual Circle." Then start filling in the Want Circle with dreams.

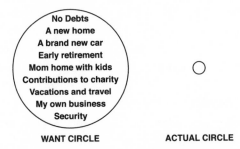

WANT CIRCLE   ACTUAL CIRCLE

For one-on-one plans: Ask the prospect what they would like to have that they won't already be able to accomplish in the next 2 to 5 years. Ask questions and get them dreaming. It may be alleviation of debt, early retirement, travel, money for charity and family, time with children, or whatever. Be sure and identify something the prospect truly wants to accomplish. Get them talking about it as much as possible.

For house plans: If possible, pick out those in the audience who appear to be the most receptive to the plan and seem to be showing the most excitement. Ask them what they would like if money and time were no object. As they give you their replies, write them in the Want Circle. Use this to get the ideas flowing for the group, and then list other dreams you know to be universal, such as those listed above for one-on-ones. At house plans, the plan presenter will have to "shot-gun" with dreams because conversations with an entire audience just won't work. Watch audience reaction as you do this, and talk more about those dreams that seem to interest your listeners the most.

Remember, you have got to help prospects identify what they want that the business can deliver or your plan will not have relevance.

Distribution Boxes

Next we move on to the second of the three intersecting trends from the beginning of the plan: Distribution. Here you draw out the conventional product distribution model.

Next, explain how Sam Walton, legendary founder of Wal-Mart, basically simplified this system and became one of the wealthiest people in the world with a company that went on to become the biggest company in the world. Explain that if Walton accomplished all of that by effectively reducing the distribution system from five steps down to four, what would happen if somebody reduced it further from four to three? How about reducing it from three to two? Or from two to one? Because that is, in effect, what the Team does! Catalog companies have done this for years, but *they* kept all the resulting savings for *themselves.* The uniqueness of what the Team does is that the money gets shared among those who make the commerce happen: in other words, the Team business owners! We call it a Consumer Rebellion. (Reference the book *Leading the Consumer Rebellion* for more explanation.) All things being equal, *we* would rather have the money than a bunch of "middle men." There is certainly nothing wrong with Wal-Mart or other retailers making money off of selling a product to a consumer – unless there were a better way. And now there is!

At this point, the plan presenter should cross out the middle boxes in the distribution chain diagram, and show product flow going *around* the cumbersome old steps in the process:

117

Then, show that the money that previously went to the "middle-men" now goes to business owners, and is split each month based upon performance.

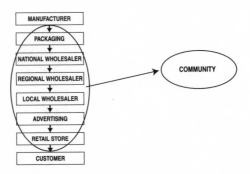

Explain how *that* is where the money comes from, the same money that supports the great dreams and lifestyles about which we have been talking. Then, explain that to make this happen, products flow in three different ways:

1. Referring others to the products (developing clients)
2. Consuming products personally (personal volume)
3. Building a community of people doing the same thing (group volume)

Through these efforts with one person or household at a time, product flow expands and multiplies as more and more people find out about the Consumer Rebellion. Who wouldn't think, "All things being equal, I'll keep the money!?" People quickly understand that money is being made every time anybody purchases something in a store. Why not cut ourselves in on the deal? That's what the Consumer Rebellion is all about: cutting ourselves in on the profits made off of us anyway!

At this point, it is also appropriate to describe exactly how we accomplish product sales and consumption. We call it our DOT1/STEP Program. *DOT1* is an acronym that stands for "Ditto On The 1st" (of the month). Explain to the prospect(s) that the *Ditto* program is like a subscription that delivers products to their door, based on their inputs, automatically. It eliminates the need for list making and manual order placing. It just happens on an easy, convenient schedule. Having the order placed automatically on the first of the month has proven the best way to help the business owner build product volume. *STEP* is another acronym that stands for "Sip Twice, Eat, and Profit." What this means is that anybody can make product flow happen in this business because everybody eats and drinks! If the business owner will simply change some of what he or she drinks (twice a day) and eats (one bar a day), he or she will be "sipping twice and eating once." This involves very little change in habits on the part of the business owner but becomes a very important duplicatable building block upon which an enormous amount of products flow. By drinking twice and eating once per day, business owners will not only be adding to their own product volume, but they will be creating numerous opportunities on a regular basis for contacting prospective new business partners or product customers. The more the products are in use and being demonstrated, the more questions and interest will result.

Don't overwhelm the prospect at this point. Just relay the simplicity of the concept of changing a little of our consumption habits on a daily basis. It may be helpful to ask questions such as, "Who doesn't drink at least twice and eat at least once per day?" "Does anybody know anyone who drinks more than twice a day and eats more than once per day?" "Great, those are excellent candidates for this program!"

Franchising and Duplication

Now the plan presenter explains the third of the intersecting trends: the Principles of Franchising. It's great that we can refer others to buy products through our business, and it's wonderful that we can consume them ourselves, but something more is needed to support the big dreams most people have listed in their Want Circles. So how do we get the business *that* big? The answer is by applying the Principles of Franchising.

The plan presenter explains how Ray Kroc, founder of McDonald's Corporation, discovered a very profitable restaurant owned by a couple of brothers who were successful but content. Kroc, however, decided the idea could be expanded around the country. Even though franchising had a very bad name at the time, and the McDonald's brothers had given up on franchising, Kroc knew a good thing when he saw it. Through the course of several years and after investing a lot of money, Kroc succeeded at making franchising work. He took the McDonald's restaurant idea and expanded it around the world, all the while pioneering a business concept that would become a mainstream idea within just a few decades.

The reason this is relevant to what the Team is doing is because we have adapted the same *principles* that allowed Kroc to succeed so enormously, except that the expensive store, food inspections, costly overhead, etc., are not required. Kroc's franchising worked because he developed a *system* to run his stores. This is the key point: instead of relying on *individuals* to run his stores, Kroc instead relied on a *proven system* to run his stores. When a *system* runs a business, *duplication* is possible. Duplication is the key to explosive business growth. If the system can run a store profitably in one location, that same system can do it in other locations. If the system and its proven techniques are followed closely, duplication from location to location produces predictable, successful results, over and over.

The plan presenter is using this example of the principles of franchising to show how proven business systems can lead to duplication and explosive growth. The Team utilizes this same concept to expand its business around the hemisphere. Where the McDonald's system is primarily interested in allowing individual store owners to operate their stores profitably, the Team is interested in helping its business owners build successful communities of people through which products and services flow. Where McDonald's has a system of how to operate a profitable fast food store, the Team's system focuses on developing the skills of building a community of people and developing wealth-thinking. This is accomplished through CD's, books, meetings, and mentorship. The plan presenter should explain each of these and how important they are in learning how to create wealth. This is also the opportunity to promote any upcoming events that may be scheduled, particularly the next Open Meeting. Finally, this training system enables *duplication* because it teaches each business owner how to succeed. The *system,* not the business owner, runs the business. The *system,* not the business owner, is available all across the hemisphere to teach details and principles. The *system* provides duplication and the power of franchising principles. *That's* how the business gets big!

Pyramids vs. the Team Building

The plan presenter has now covered each of the three intersecting trends that were introduced at the beginning of the plan. Next, it is time to explain what the Team business *is,* and what it is *not.*

The presenter should begin this phase by drawing out what many people think is a "pyramid scheme." This is a convenient time during the talk to overcome that concern. Explain a little about what an illegal pyramid scheme is, and then explain how this business differs.

For example, illegal qualities which make a pyramid:
- Upfront product loading
- Making money by recruiting others to join ("headhunter rewards")
- Those who get in first make more money than those who get in later

121

However, the Team doesn't have up front product loading, nor do we make money by "recruiting" others to join. Also, anybody can make more than anybody else; the money doesn't go to those who "got in" first. Further, when someone is not interested in becoming a business owner on the Team, we give them the opportunity to become a *customer*. By turning "no's" into customers, our plan showing helps us generate retail product volume.

Contrast these notions of "pyramid businesses" to the Team's *Team Approach* method of building communities. Help the prospect(s) understand that they will be in business *for* themselves but not *by* themselves. They will be part of a team; they will have help. (For more in-depth information about Team Approach, consult the book, *Leading the Consumer Rebellion*). This section of the plan is the opportunity for the plan presenter to distinguish the Team from every other business opportunity out there, both good and bad. It is also a good time to talk about the up-line and the leaders of the Team, creating the respect for what has been achieved and the desire for the prospects to attend a meeting where they can meet these people.

As you draw out the concept of depth, show circles to represent business owners joining the team. Then explain how each of these business owners will be "Sipping Twice a day and Eating Once," or at least handing out two drinks and one bar a day or even retailing them! Help the prospect(s) see the tremendous potential for product flow that results from a team of people each doing a simple, duplicatable step of moving products. The only qualification is being able to eat and drink, or at least finding others to supply who eat and drink on a regular basis!

Finally, show how at first the biggest thing that helps people understand the business is *information*. Tell the prospect(s) that they will be provided CD's and books and pamphlets for this very purpose (as will be explained in the next section). But then, there is another, more powerful way for someone to get convinced of the merits of the business, namely, *progress*. As your team works together to expand *their* team, they will see first-hand proof that this business works because they will be seeing progress. Finally, though, the most convincing step is *income*. As products flow through the team you will build together, income will flow to the deserving participants and will finish the job of convincing them that the business is for them. Explain that the three part program of *information, progress, and income* will bring them up to speed as an excited business owner.

After the Plan

There is a natural tendency to feel good at the end of showing a plan, and it is tempting to skip the final touches that make it all worthwhile. Resist that temptation. Be a professional and complete the job thoroughly and properly.

Regarding one-on-ones: Ask the prospect if he or she has any questions. Answer them very briefly, and if at all possible, refer them to the first-night materials you will be leaving them as a source for their answers. Use the *First-Night Pack* (and make sure the SA 4400 brochure is included). Promote each of the materials and create the hunger for the prospect to review them. Handing them out is not enough. We must put an emphasis on the materials that will make the prospect want to review them. Next, tell the prospect why you think he or she would be good at the business, and let them know you would like to work with them. If they want to "hold their spot" on the Team at this point, they certainly can, but it is not critical that this take place the first night. (Much more important than "signing them up" is to get them to review the first-night materials and attend the next available Open Meeting.) Take out your calendar and schedule a time to get back together with the prospect(s) and answer any of their questions. Tell them that tonight you have explained *what* the business is, and when you get back together you will cover the *how* side of actually building it. The best time to get back together for the follow-through is within two days. Any longer than that and the prospect loses interest. As the saying goes, "Time kills all interest." Do not leave their house without booking a follow-through appointment!

Regarding house plans: When the plan-presenter is married and his wife is present, it is helpful for her to share for 5-10 minutes at the end of the plan. The purpose is simply to show a different perspective that might better relate to some of the spouses in the room. She should relate an objection or two that she had when they first got started and how they were overcome. A possible example would be, "I remember when I first saw this business, it was like taking a drink from a fire hose. It was so much new information and I was skeptical! Going to the Open Meeting like the one this Tuesday really helped me understand it better. I didn't know how we could possibly have time to do anything else in our lives; we are so busy. Now I see how we would never have had any more time if we had kept doing what we were doing; but I see people who have been doing this who have time to stay home with their kids, go on a vacation every month and be debt free. I'm excited to be involved and we invite you to join us."

After the plan (and after the wife's comments if applicable), the host of the meeting should be brought to the board to share some closing comments. The objective here is for the host to reiterate how excited he or she is about the business and to express commitment to doing it. This is also a great opportunity to compliment the speaker on a job well done. Appropriate closing remarks are short and enthusiastic. Possible examples might be, "Now you can all see why (spouse) and I are so excited about this business. (Speaker) did a great job of explaining it, and we appreciate him (or her) coming tonight. We have decided to move ahead with this business full speed, and we are delighted that you've had a chance to see what we are so excited about. We would love to work with you in the business if you determine that it's for you, too! We have some samples of our Sports/Nutrition products in the kitchen if you'd like to try them, and we can take some time individually to answer any questions you may have. Also, (plan presenter) has agreed to stick around to help answer any questions. Also, for those of you who would like to learn how to get started, stick around. In a few minutes we'll gather back in this room. For those of you that can't stay, drive safe." These comments, or something very similar, are the most appropriate. **It is *not* appropriate to thank the audience for coming.** If they understand the value of what they just saw, they will thank the host for inviting them! **Also, it is not appropriate to open the meeting up for questions and answers at the end.** Break up the meeting, get the crowd into the kitchen, or some other mingling spot, and let questions be addressed individually there.

The presenter of the house plan should then mingle with the crowd, picking out the most excited prospects, giving them first-night materials, and booking individual follow through appointments with them, in much the same manner as described for a one-on-one. The host and any other up-line present may want to do the same things with the other prospects.

Regarding both one-on-ones and house plans: **The plan presenter should *never* leave the house without booking a follow-through.** Also, once booking the follow through, then it is appropriate to invite the prospect to the next Open Meeting. It is usually a good idea to offer to pick them up and take them to the Open. They are more likely to come if you bring them. It is best to book a follow-through even when they are planning to attend the Open Meeting. The two are very different activities, and if the prospect misses the Open, you are forced to call them and "chase" them down, as we discussed before. To avoid this issue, simply book the follow-through first, then arrange to have them attend the Open Meeting.

At the end of either house plans or one-on-ones, it is a good idea to present product samples. Give them a can or two of your favorite energy drink flavor, and one of the bars. (At house meetings, it is best to have sample drinks in small cups and the bars cut into pieces). This brings a solidity to the business, and besides, many people who don't necessarily grasp the concepts of a business right away *do* get excited by the quality and potential of our products.

To complete a house plan properly, whoever closes the "plan" portion of the presentation should state (as referred to above), "For anybody who would like to learn how to get started, stick around. After we have refreshments and try some of the products, we'll get back together really quickly and listen to (up-line's name) show us how to get started." This second part of the meeting is to be conducted by the highest level, most successful, most committed leader in the room. The speaker should walk the new people through the importance of the system, attending the next event, and preparing to get the business in front of the people that *they* know. This section should not involve too much detailed teaching, but rather the posture and conviction that the prospects have made the right choice and have joined the right team. This part of the presentation should finish the job of getting the prospects interested in the business. At the end of this portion, prospects can sign up right on the spot, but it is not critical. They will be walking out the door with materials, an appointment booked for someone to get back with them and start moving their business along, and a date for an Open Meeting near them. In effect, they are "in." They should also know when the next time this group is getting together to do a house meeting, and they should be thinking about whom they would like to bring to it.

Go-Getter

We have gone through the details of showing the plan. Now let's talk a little bit about the pace of the business, in other words, how often one shows the plan.

The Power Player Program states that Power Players show the plan themselves a minimum of fifteen times in a month. This is a very critical activity level that has been proven over and over again. It is okay to start slower than that and ramp up, but understand the importance of working up to a level of activity that allows your business a chance to gain momentum and prosper. Showing fifteen plans a month can be compared to treading water. There is a certain amount of arm and leg strokes that keep the swimmer afloat; anything less, even a *little* less, and the swimmer is not a swimmer for long! Fifteen plans works much the same way. It is a level of activity that not only keeps the business owner's business afloat, but propels it forward. Less than that on a consistent basis will lead to some sinking. For that reason, Power Players show at least fifteen plans a month. Those business owners who show that plan at that pace are called Go-Getters and are recognized at the monthly seminars.

Summary

For your business to grow, it will be necessary to become adept at showing the plan yourself. In the beginning, your up-line will show plans on your behalf. This is to help you get started growing a business and to demonstrate how it is done. Eventually, you will take over showing plans to grow your own business. The good news is that this is one of the most interesting and enjoyable steps in the entire business. People are diverse and fun to meet, and as you show the plan you will collect relationships and stories that will warm your heart, make you laugh, and build a big business.

Personal Story

Names: Mike and Carol Foos
Former Occupations: Mechanical Engineer; Orthodontic Technician

In 2001, they were a family that was very "time poor." He had an Engineering degree and a Masters in Business, and had spent the last 24 years of his life in corporate America. At that time, he was a manager for a large automotive company, had a company car and a nice six-figure income. She had worked in the dental field as an orthodontic technician for 17 years and loved her profession, yet wanted more time with her family as well. They were financially flat-lined, over-worked, and stressed, always wondering how to change something in their lives. They couldn't imagine doing the same thing for 20 more years!

While volunteering at her daughters' elementary school, Carol met Lynette, who told her that she and her husband Ed had an Internet company that enabled her to leave her job and become a stay-at-home mom. Carol went home and told Mike what Lynette had said. Shortly thereafter, they saw Ed working on the subdivision sprinkler system. Mike approached Ed with the question, "I heard you had an Internet company, is it Amway?" Ed answered "No, but I can show you what it is!" They sat down with Ed, and the information he shared about Robert Kiyosaki's Cashflow Quadrant and the "45 year plan" most of us are living was shocking! After so many years of corporate experience and an MBA degree, Mike wondered how he and Carol could have missed this information!

The next night, they went to a Tuesday night Open Meeting. That sealed the decision! The posture and belief that came through that night was what did it. These were real people on stage, with similar backgrounds, and they had achieved what Mike and Carol were looking for. It is because of this impact of attending an Open Meeting that Mike and Carol are such strong proponents of getting new people to Open Meetings. They realize that giving someone a chance to see the bigger picture, to pick up the feeling of possibility and success, and to see a crowd of excited, goal-directed people all aiming for the same great lifestyle, is priceless for someone truly looking for a way to change his or her life financially. Getting good at getting people to Open Meetings became just one of the many areas in the business at which Mike and Carol decided to excel. And it has always remained a prominent feature in their business building strategy.

Life has radically changed for Mike and Carol's family. With the guidance of their mentors Tim and Amy, and the help of Ed and Lynette (along with numerous educational, motivational, and encouraging experiences given by the Woodwards and Bradys), they are now "job optional," having replaced their incomes after just 29 months! They have time to be stay-at-home parents, give to charities, and travel whenever and wherever they want. They love this business because they have a vehicle to help others achieve their goals and dreams while living theirs! "It can happen for you too", they say. "It all comes down to Having Fun, Making Money, and Making a Difference in the lives of others! There's no better way to live."

"The only time evil can flourish is when good men do nothing."
- Edmond Burke

"It is not enough to be busy, so too are the ants. The question is; what are we busy about?"
- Henry David Thoreau

"Don't worry about whether you're better than somebody else, but never cease trying to be the best you can become. You have control over that; the other you don't."
- John Wooden

"Everything comes to him who hustles while he waits."
- Thomas Edison

"I can accept failure, everyone fails at something. But I can't accept not trying."
- Michael Jordan

Name: NEGATIVE NANCY

Quote: "How much money are you making? You know all those things are scams. My uncle's, doctor's, daughter got into one of those things, and she lost everything."

Chapter 7

Activity, Part Three
Following Through and Rotating the Pattern

After showing the plan, the remaining steps in the Five Step Pattern are:

4. Following-Through
5. Rotating the Pattern – Getting Them Started

The previous step, showing the plan, was intended not to "sign them up," but primarily to get the prospective new business owner involved in the training system. It is much more important to have someone involved in the system (i.e. listening to CD's, reading books, and attending meetings) and *not* signed up than it is to have them signed up and *not* involved in the system. This is because success in the Information Age requires one to acquire and apply the correct *information*. Signing someone up accomplishes nothing in terms of teaching them wealth-thinking. However, involving them in the training system introduces them to a whole world of wealth training information. It is such information that is leveraged to build a strong and profitable business.

In the Information Age, the battleground is in each of our minds. Those with the correct information win. Those without it, for instance, those stuck in Industrial Age thinking, lose. Therefore, it is of the utmost importance to involve all new potential business owners in the training system as soon as possible. It is like being sure a horse dying of thirst gets to water quickly. There will be enough time later for attending to the details of bridles and saddles. Signing up a new business owner is a bridle and saddle activity. It is surely important, but only after the horse is nourished.

Following Through

We begin this chapter with this discussion about leading prospective business owners to the training system because that is exactly what the follow-through step is really all about. To learn more about this part of the process, be sure to consult the many audio CD's that teach this topic in depth.

The main components of *following-through* are:

1. Re-Familiarize Them With Their Dream
2. Answer Questions
3. Overcome Objections
4. Involve them in the System
5. Begin Rotating the Pattern on their Behalf
6. Continue Building a Relationship

Re-Familiarize Them With Their Dream

Between the time a person sees the plan and their follow-through, many things can happen. Usually, prospective business owners have asked other people for their opinions about the business. While it should be obvious that those *uninvolved* with the business and most likely *not financially successful* are not valuable sources of assessment, it is a natural tendency for all of us to bounce ideas off people we know. As a result of this, the prospective business owner might have received negative feedback. Simply be prepared to handle it. The best way to be prepared is to be thoroughly involved in the training system yourself, so that you have the information to counter any misconceptions that may be out there. Then, understand that nobody really wants to *do* the business, the only reason anybody gets involved is for what they can *accomplish* through the "doing" of the business. Nobody wants something else to *do*; what they want is a better lifestyle. Obviously, the business is one of the best ways to accomplish a better lifestyle, and that is what should be emphasized at the follow-through step. This is what we call re-familiarizing them with their dream.

Specifically, it is a good idea to draw out a circle on a piece of paper, and ask the prospective business owner to refresh your memory as to what they would like to achieve in the next two to five years if money and time were not an object. This step is designed to get them focused on the dream again. Remember, the only reason anybody gets involved in the business is "what's in it for them." It is critical at the follow-through step to drive this point home. We quoted Carl Sandburg in Chapter 1 as saying, "Nothing happens without first a dream." We could modify that saying for our business: "Nothing will happen *in the Team business* without first a dream." Because of that, it is of primary importance to help the prospect remember that the whole thing they are considering when looking at the Team business is whether or not they really want their dreams. Let's face it, without a vehicle like the Team business, most people will not experience the majority of their goals and dreams. As one man said, "They will die with their music still in them." Therefore, the question isn't, "Do you want to participate in the Team business?" but rather "Do you want your dreams?" The Team business simply plugs people into a way to get their dreams. The analogy is the buying of a power drill. Does the buyer really want a drill, or does he or she want a hole? The drill is simply a tool to provide the end result the buyer actually wants. The Team business is the same way.

Answer Questions

The most natural thing that will happen at a follow-through is for the prospective business owner to have some questions. Be sure and spend the time required to help the prospect understand the business by providing the best information you can. This is why it is so important to be involved in the training system yourself so that you will have the answers and the confidence to provide those answers.

However, the very best way to answer questions is by using the training system itself. Instead of becoming the answerer to every question, allow the training system to answer the questions. What do we mean by this? Well, what if someone asked a question regarding the legality of the business? A correct way to answer this would be to hand them a copy of one of the CD's in the system that addresses that very question. You could even promote the CD by saying, "Here's my brief version of the answer to that question, but I'm no lawyer. On this CD right here, a very distinguished lawyer gives his analysis of our business. It has a lot more detail than I could give you. Your question is answered on this CD." In this way, you become the *messenger* and not the *message*. You become a doorway to the information and not the source of information yourself. The most effective business owners understand that they must rely upon the system to teach their partners instead of themselves.

Overcome Objections

People building the business sometimes get hung up on what they should do or say when prospective business owners have objections of some kind. The first thing to realize is that objections to something new are quite normal. If you think back, you probably had an objection or two to getting involved in the business. Considered in this way, objections may even be a sign of sincere interest in learning more about the business. After all, nobody takes the time to offer up objections for something in which he has no interest.

There is a difference, however, between an objection and an excuse. An objection is a legitimate concern that if properly addressed with information, will go away and clear the path for progress. Excuses are annoying little things that if addressed, will only give birth to another. That is how you can tell the difference between a sincere objection and an excuse.

Author Frank Bettger wrote about a way to distinguish between an objection and an excuse. Instead of addressing an objection (or excuse) head on, Bettger said to simply ask the question, "Besides that, would there be anything *else* that would hold you back?" If the reply is another reason, then the first reason offered was not really an objection, but an excuse. This could continue through several excuses. Finally, by repeatedly asking that same question, you will arrive at a point where there are no more excuses. The *last* thing holding up the prospect is the real objection. All others before that were simply excuses.

Diamond, Larry VanBusKirk has another way of accomplishing the same thing. His question is, "Oh really, why is that?" (It should be noted, however, that Larry claims this is much more effective if pronounced as we will spell it here phonetically: "ORE-ALLY WHYZAT?") Repeating this question a few times ought to drive at the real reason.

Use either approach. The goal is to get to the real objection so time can be spent finding a real solution or work-around and not wasting it chopping away at fake excuses.

Another good way to deal with objections people have, because many are just fears or lack of information, is to follow the formula of Feel, Felt, and Found. If you are offered an objection for which the statement rings true, you can respond with, "I know how you *feel*, I *felt* the same way, but here's what I *found*...." Again, make sure you are sincere, and don't use this simply as some type of tactic on someone. But if you truly did feel that way, empathize with their position first, then let them know what information or perspective was helpful to you in getting past the objection.

As you gain experience building the business, you will discover that of all the people you will run across out there, most of them share the same two or three concerns about getting started in the Team business. The problem, eventually, will not be knowing what to say or how to respond. It will be that you have too many pieces of information to give in reply! The problem will be choosing which is most appropriate!

Involve Them in the System

We have been making this point over and over. The whole goal of these early moments in the experience of a new business owner is to lead them to the information that has the potential to help them get their dreams. Each step of the way this is accomplished through CD's, books, pamphlets, and involvement in meetings.

At the follow-through step, invitations should be made to the next meeting, and more informational materials should be left with them for their review. Be sure to "promote" each piece of material you loan them by pointing out its specific relevance to their situation. "You will love this CD, it's by a husband and wife who were both teachers, just like you and your spouse," etc. Or, "This book goes through the exact details it takes to build your leadership skills, just like you were asking." You have to create a hunger on the part of the prospect to delve deeper into the information.

Another way to do this is to tie things back to their dream. For instance, you might encounter someone who is hesitant to invest the time or money to attend an upcoming seminar. You must help them see the *value* in attending. Remember: always help them see "what's in it for them." Your promotion of the event might go like this: "Bob, I know you wanted more detailed information on how to build your community, and this upcoming seminar is going to do just that. They'll lay out all the information in a very learnable format and you'll come out of there with a much clearer idea of how to build your business to the point of being able to afford that log cabin you want to build." The key axiom is this: don't ever try to *get* people to *do* anything. Try to help them get what they want by doing what is necessary. The Team business owners are sort of like a "Merit" Santa Claus. They give people a way to get what they want.

Begin Rotating the Pattern on Their Behalf

The reason we call this step in the pattern "follow-through" instead of "follow-up" is because we are most interested in continuing the process before it's even really begun. This may sound confusing, but allow us to explain.

We could go through all the work of trying to help someone become convinced to participate as a business owner, get them "signed up," etc. We could spend hours and hours answering their questions. But a much more effective way to help them get a feel for the business is to simply give it a try. It's a lot like a new car dealership that allows prospective customers to "test drive" a new vehicle before making a purchasing decision. The best way for someone to understand the business is by giving it a "test drive." We can easily help them show the plan to someone *they* know, even before they are officially business owners themselves. We can do this before they've attended any events, *and* we can do this before they've even listened to any recordings or reviewed any literature.

Many times upon seeing the plan, people become excited. They begin thinking of people with whom they'd like to share the idea. Remember as we said before, it is natural for people to want to go out and solicit opinions about the business anyway. Why not do it the *correct* way? Why not go out and solicit opinions with *you*, one who can show the plan, there to help them? In this way, it goes from a function of collecting opinions to a process of showing the plan to more people. This process can begin as soon as you are done showing the plan. You can suggest that the idea could be bounced off some other people immediately, depending on the prospect's schedule. "How's right now?" you might ask. Sometimes this works, sometimes it doesn't. But it doesn't hurt to ask. If the prospect can't or won't lead you to anybody else immediately, sometimes they *can* by the next day or so. Great. This initiates the Five Step Pattern all over again, and effectively becomes what we term "building depth," which is a concept we'll highlight in Chapter 8.

Sometimes, however, the prospective new business owner is not ready to begin talking to his or her friends right away. In those cases, we should conduct the follow-through by initiating the Five Step Pattern on their behalf. First, once answering their questions, loaning them more training materials, and inviting and promoting them to the next meeting, we can begin helping them with Step 1: Making a Names List. This does not have to be an exhaustive exercise, but it is normally liberating for the prospect. This is because with the help of a memory jogger pamphlet, the *Who Do You Know* brochure, the prospect can rather quickly generate a large list of names. This becomes exciting for them as they realize they know a lot of people and the odds are pretty good many of them will be interested in the Team business. By taking the first step, we are also gently walking them into the business by showing them that they *can do* the activity and that we will be there to help them.

Depending on how well the making of the names list goes, we can next encourage the prospect to move to Step 2 of the Five Step Pattern and contact a few people on the list. This takes us back to what we were doing above when we decided to just show the plan to the people the prospect would solicit opinions from anyway. At this point, we are trying to get the prospect to make a formal appointment with those on his or her names list. It is crucial to sit there with them and help on this step, although many will say they'd rather do it alone later. Either way, be sure to prep them on at least the basic principles of contacting before they begin, but don't overwhelm them or "over train."

Helping the prospect take these initial steps of the Five Step Pattern may not happen all at one meeting. It may take several visits to get them moving through these steps. For instance, you might answer their questions and leave them some more material at the first follow-through appointment. Then they attend an Open Meeting, and you get back together the next day. **Always remember to book a meeting from a meeting**. Now they are ready to make their names list, but not ready to contact anybody yet. Give them some more materials and pick another time to get back with them. At that stage, it will likely be time to begin contacting and scheduling their first house plan. All of this is okay. As long as they are showing sincere interest and not just wasting your time, allow the process to move along at a pace that is at least a little comfortable for them. However, your time is valuable, too. And it is all a balance. You don't want to be rushing the process along at such a pace that they feel overwhelmed or "pushed" into doing anything. On the other hand, you can't make trip after trip to meet with a prospect that isn't really taking action in the business. In each case, this will be a judgment call on your part. The trick is to get your calendar as full as you want it with appointments with other people, so that you really only have time for those who are the hungriest. Remember, the hungriest people in life are the ones that succeed the biggest, and that's exactly who we are looking for through this whole process. So don't push people too fast, but don't let them waste your time (or theirs), either.

Continue Building a Relationship

Our business is one of relationships. In fact, most businesses are; that's what Michael Dell meant by "building communities." But perhaps no business runs on relationships as much as the Team business. For that reason, it is vitally important to remember, always, that relationships are more important than tasks. We should never get so caught up in the Five Step Pattern, or the objectives of what we are trying to accomplish in the follow-through step, or promoting the next seminar, or any other task, that we lose site of the *relationships*. People come before tasks. It's the most important part of our business, and, for that matter, the most important part of life. As the saying goes, "We are here to serve other people."

We discussed building relationships in the section on showing the plan. The principles are exactly the same for the follow-through step. Take an interest in the other person. Learn to listen, and by all means, do not be an "over-talker." Be sincere. Try to find common ground. Be real, open, and honest. In short, become a friend.

Every step of the business, from the initial contact to showing the plan, to following through, to attending events, to phone calls, are all opportunities for building a tighter relationship with those with whom we are building the business. Take every activity in the business as a chance to build a tighter bond with people. As one successful business owner once said, "I try to go around sprinkling a little bit of sunshine everywhere I go."

Signing Them Up

Okay, now we can talk about "signing them up." When is the most appropriate time to do it? As soon as the prospective business owner is ready. Many, many times, this can happen immediately at the end of the plan.

There is a school of thought on why this is a good idea. Basically, if a person commits a little bit of money to something, he or she will immediately start feeling some ownership, or will basically feel like an insider. Then when he or she goes through the first-night information, it is for "their" business, not someone else's. They become an advocate, not an investigator.

It is just as common, however, for a sign-up to happen at the first follow-through step. Or, it may take several follow-through meetings until this occurs.

Whether a prospect signs up right away or not is up to them. But the part that is up to you, the one who shows the plan, is to ask for their commitment. In other words, ask them to join the team. As said before, there is usually an increase in commitment to something once somebody has committed some of their money to it. For that reason, it matters that they eventually do sign up. The best way to get this to happen is to ask for it. At the end of the plan, once the initial questions have been answered, you might pose the question, "So, are you guys ready to hold your spot on the Team?" or "I'd love to have you guys on the Team with us. Are you ready to become official as a business owner?" or "I think we've got a good match here. Can I officially welcome you to the Team (extending your hand across the table for a handshake)?" Another phrase Tim Marks has popularized is, "Do you want to know why most people I show this to join the team on the spot? (pause) It's because there is little or no risk; it's 'anyway money' with our DOT1/STEP program (money that you'll be spending 'anyway'), and you can do as little or as much as you want." Whichever of these methods you use to ask the prospect to join the Team, your next step (and it is the toughest part) is to sit quietly and let them decide. Don't fill the air with words. Wait for their reply. If their answer is, "No. Not yet," you can dig into their reason why (see the section a couple of pages back entitled **Overcoming Objections**). If you can't turn around their objections (and don't push too hard here, remember, signing them up is not the main objective) then just say, "great" and continue with the process of leaving materials and booking the follow-through (or next follow-through). If it is, "yes," then just say, "great," and pull out the appropriate forms for them to fill out and collect payment, followed by booking the follow-through (or next follow-through).

During the step where the new business owner is filling out the paperwork, be sure and promote to them the additional materials and information they may want to purchase to help their business get off to a fast start. Find out from your up-line what materials are most appropriate for this. Remember, signing them up is not nearly as important as giving them the information they need to succeed. Help them understand the value in this, and write it up as a separate order.

Also, if you have not already done so at that meeting, it is a good idea to give them more product samples. This will get them excited about the first shipment of product samples they will be receiving which they can then hand out to others. Don't be stingy with your product samples; they are your cheapest and most effective form of advertising!

Preventing Overload

Guard yourself against giving people drinks of water through a fire hose. It is sometimes a tendency among business owners to overwhelm prospects with too much information. The important principle to remember is "What's Important Next." There are many, many great things to tell the prospect about the business, but all in due time. Be careful to focus only upon what is most important for their success at that point in the journey. The prospects or new business owners can learn all about the details of various things later as they become more familiar with their new venture. It is your job to help them focus on the one or two most important things to do next, and prevent overload. You will only be able to do this if you become capable of "reading" people a little bit. Learn to look for the signs of disinterest or fatigue. Look for indications that certain things excite them more than others. Again, as with so many aspects of this business, the better you know people and how to deal with them, the better off you'll be.

Rotating the Pattern – Getting Them Started

Rotating the pattern has really already been discussed. If you do step four, follow-through, properly, you will begin initiating the new business owners in the process of exposing the business idea to new people. By helping them make a list, show the plan, and follow through with those people, you are helping them rotate the pattern and in fact doing the fifth step in the pattern!

Guess what you do when the prospect (or new business owner) leads you to some people who have dreams and are looking? The exact same thing. Now you help *them* rotate the pattern to find the people *they* know that are looking. This is really the beginning of the discussion of the concept of "building depth," which we will discuss in the next chapter.

But let's say that you do all the steps in the process properly, and someone still isn't interested in getting involved in the business as a business owner. Now what do you do? We like to help business owners understand that when you rotate this pattern, at the end of it, only two things will happen:

1. You get a new business partner on your team or
2. You get a new customer.

If it turns out that the business isn't for a particular prospect (because as we like to say, this business isn't for *everyone*), then the next step should be to turn him or her into a customer. With world-class products, why wouldn't someone want to take advantage of what we have to offer for at least some of their buying needs? Who doesn't want to be a bit more healthy, have a bit more energy, or lose a few more pounds? Our Sports/Nutrition line is perfect for all of these purposes and more! That's where you come in. You have spent at least a little time with this prospect. You have built rapport with them (hopefully). You have started a relationship, or perhaps you already had one with that person. Making him or her a customer is a natural next step. People sometimes ask us, "Where and how do I find my retail customers?" One way is through the efforts you are expending toward building your community. You've invested time and energy in this prospect; now finish it off with some retail volume. Doing so is also a great way to stay in touch with a prospect, to keep him or her thinking about your business, and it provides a window into your forthcoming success. Often it happens that people at first say "no" to the business and simply become customers; later, they get interested in business ownership, because of what they see changing in the life of the person who showed them the plan. Also, other people take an interest in the products they see the customer using, and it helps show the customer that the business could work for them! This just might bring them back to you as a business partner some day down the road.

Even more to the point, this business ultimately comes down to product flow. Even though the focus of this book is on the *community building* aspect of our business, another enormous component is *retailing*. Remember, we are building a community through which products and services flow. The more retail volume a new business owner can generate, the sooner he or she will be profitable, and the higher those profits will be. So take advantage of the work you've already done in the Five Step Pattern and learn to turn your "no's" into customers.

Personal Story

Names: Larry and Marsie VanBuskirk
Former Occupations: Business Owner and Financial
Consultant; Wife/Mother

As a former financial planner and business consultant, I felt that I had a pretty good grasp on what it took to set up and operate a business. I certainly was far above considering any serious participation in an "at home" type of business, although Marsie was quite serious about the concept.

In keeping with my foresight in the area of technological change, I left the financial field and founded a substantial communications business – in pay telephones. The payphone business was red-hot at the time, and started on a very prosperous note. Then enter cellular phones! We ignored the obvious change taking place, and ploughed on in a less and less stable industry until the day all our money and our business was gone.

Simply, at age fifty, I moved from relatively prosperous CEO status to serious debt, no income and extreme embarrassment. Our only stable income seemed to come from a small amount per month from that "at home" business Marsie had started.

With the advent of the Internet, I got excited about the possibility of expanding that small income into a substantial business income. Unfortunately, my business training had not extended to the concept of willing teams working in unison toward a common goal, but was more in the realm of John Maxwell's "positional authority," where one gives orders and they are carried out under threat of job displacement. Even with a good amount of time invested, success seemed further than "just around the corner" doing things my way.

In desperation, I decided to listen to and accept the mentorship of a younger man with much more wisdom than I. Orrin Woodward introduced me to the concepts embodied in the Team, and the leadership principles that the Team teaches and stands for. After continuing for a time to "merge" his concepts into my way, I finally fully accepted him as my mentor.

The results over the past five years have been more than spectacular! As a servant leader, we were able to accomplish things that I would have deemed impossible in corporate America. We have gone from an almost impossible debt burden to no debt whatsoever. Our income has reached heights that I had not even fantasized possible. We have attained a level of respect from our peers that I had always dreamed of. And all of this was accomplished, not by manipulating people to my advantage, but by helping people discover their strengths and talents through the most effective leadership development training system I have ever experienced! We have developed friendships and great relationships with thousands of people I would never have met, and I know we have positively impacted their lives. We have been privileged to develop teams in several countries (the Bahamas, Puerto Rico, Canada), and all over the United States, so we are also able to experience our lifetime dream of extensive travel. What a wonderful way to live, learn, and impact society we have experienced through the grace of God, and the wonderful concept of the Team!

"Don't stand shivering upon the bank; plunge in at once, and have it over with."
- Sam Glick

"Work is more fun than fun."
- Noel Coward

"The harder I work the luckier I get."
- Thomas Jefferson

"The world is full of willing people. Some willing to work, the rest willing to let them."
- Robert Frost

"Some who are not paid what they are worth ought to be glad."
- unknown

Name: NED THE KNOW-IT-ALL
Quote: "That's a neat little idea you
got, but you're doing it all
wrong. Let me tell you how
to fix that so you can make
some REAL money. "

Chapter 8

Results
Depth Is Not an Option

In this book we have already covered a lot of ground. We've discussed dreams and wealth-thinking, introduced the Power Player Program, and talked through the Theory and Activity portions of the program. Now it is time to learn about *Results*. We need to know what kind of results to shoot for, and how to measure them. Understanding theory is great. Doing the activity required for success is wonderful. But we must follow a specific strategy and then measure how we are doing to keep our business on track toward our goals and dreams.

The Theory of Depth

Every successful business enterprise must have a key strategy that makes everything work. Author Robert Kiyosaki calls it the "tactic that all strategies are based upon." Author Jim Collins calls it "the hedgehog concept." Name it what you will, the message is the same. In order to thrive, a business must have a core competency, an advantage that is utilized to accomplish success.

In the Team business, that core competency is the concept of "building depth." This is a deep subject (pun intended; we couldn't resist), but well worth digging into (sorry). Depth is the condition where one business owner registers or signs up another business owner into his business. In the business relationship that results, a bond is formed. As each new business owner registers onto the Team, or as more bonds are formed in depth, or "under" the previous business owner, "depth" is the result. See the diagram below.

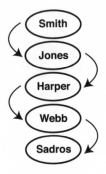

Depth accomplishes many things in the health of your organization. Included in these are:

1. Providing proof to new business owners
2. Building large numbers of people into your organization
3. Providing the best leverage for your time
4. Producing a secure business

Providing Proof to New Business Owners

Depth is important for many reasons. One main reason is that people need a little proof that the business is real and that it actually works. As they see depth develop underneath them, they begin to believe that a large organization could be the result of continuing such growth. This increased belief increases their excitement, which normally increases their activity level, which increases the speed at which they do the work to grow their business, which increases their belief, etc. A simpler way of putting it is that depth is the wedge that drives open the door of momentum. Once depth begins happening consistently and quickly enough in an organization, that group takes off at astounding growth rates. Everybody gets excited, people join the organization at a furious rate, and the resulting product flow becomes enormous. As that product flow increases, the business owner qualifies for higher and higher rebates from the products he or she consumes or sells themselves, because of achieving a higher and higher position on the performance bonus chart. This also, obviously, adds to the excitement and belief. As we discussed before, if *information* gets a person interested in the business in the beginning, *progress* increases that interest. Building depth demonstrates progress. Finally, as the organization grows, *income* solidifies that interest into belief!

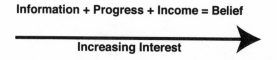

Information + Progress + Income = Belief

Increasing Interest

Building Large Numbers of People into your Organization

Depth is the most effective method for building large numbers of people in a community. The deeper an organization becomes, the more exponential the growth of the numbers. To cause an explosion in the numbers of people involved in the business, **build depth.**

Providing the Best Leverage for Your Time

Depth also is a mighty form of time leveraging. Imagine an organization where there was no depth, but only something called "width." In such an organization, the leading business owner would have to "split" his or her time up among each new participant in the business in order to help them all. This is a division of time and effort and a dilution of energy, at best. One hour given assisting a new business partner results in one hour given. But

153

with depth, an hour given to assist someone deep within an organization has the effect of helping everybody "above" that person in the line of sponsorship. If you were to work in a location ten levels in depth below yourself, and contribute an hour of your time, you would effectively gain ten hours worth of result!

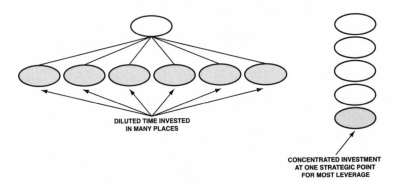

DILUTED TIME INVESTED
IN MANY PLACES

CONCENTRATED INVESTMENT
AT ONE STRATEGIC POINT
FOR MOST LEVERAGE

Producing a Secure Business

Depth also produces security. As an organization gets deeper and deeper, it has an increased ability to hold people together as a strong team. This is because so many people are in a position of potentially making money. With such a large group established "under" them, the potential for incomes becomes enormous. This is because of the sheer numbers involved. All that is required for someone with one deep organization to begin producing larger and larger incomes is to capitalize on the growth by duplicating that example in another, second organization. This applies again with a third, and eventually a fourth organization, and so on.

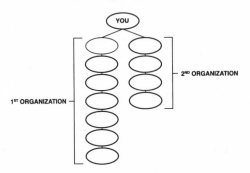

The Specifics of Depth

Understanding that depth is important, and that it is the key to developing a large community of people through which products and services flow, is one thing. Learning *how* to build it is another.

Building depth is not complicated. In fact, it is very simple. To do it, simply contact someone, show him or her the plan, and help him or her lead you to someone else to show the plan to, then repeat the process over and over again. We discussed this heavily in the previous chapter, but perhaps a diagram will be helpful.

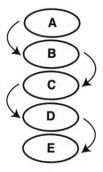

First, show the plan to Person (or Couple) A. As you follow the Five Step Pattern in your dealings with Person A, he or she will lead you to Person B. Person B then leads you to Person C, and so on.

Team Approach

Team Approach is the name for the master strategy in the Team business when a group of people get together and focus on building depth at the bottom of an organization. The combined efforts of several business owners helping everybody at the bottom to grow the business "deeper" can result in faster growth and more momentum for everybody in the leg. This is because even if one business owner doesn't achieve results in depth a certain day, one of the other business owners assisting in the bottom of the organization may. The Team Approach to the business results in faster growth than if it were being done by just a lone individual business owner.

Master the Pattern

To become good at building depth in an organization, one must master the Five Step Pattern. The way to master something is to study the theory, and repeatedly apply the theory to actual practice. Listen to the CD's relating to the pattern, read through the literature, and show the plan as much and as often as you can. Do this over and over. Proficiency comes through repetition. It may also help you to memorize key phrases that you find useful in each of the five steps. Consult your up-line or mentor to analyze your performance and make adjustments.

There is nothing complicated about rotating the Five Step Pattern. In fact, anyone with basic faculties can do it. Making a list simply involves writing down some names. Contacting people simply means calling someone. Showing the plan simply means to have a conversation. Following through means to have an additional conversation. Rotating the pattern on their behalf is a repeat of what you've just done. Everybody can do these steps, but those who choose to do them repeatedly, and to the point of getting good at them, will have the biggest and fastest growing businesses. This also means that they will make the most money!

Being Bad to Get Good

To get good at something, you normally have to start out by being bad at it, first. That's okay. All things worth doing well are worth doing badly until you can learn to do them well. And the only reason you may not be great at these steps at first is because it is new to you. Chances are, you weren't a star performer your first day on your job, either. A certain amount of time was required to get acquainted with the surroundings, learn what was expected of you, and to gain proficiency. The Team business will be no different. Give yourself time to get good at it; because the Team business can work so well that it just might be the last thing you'll ever have to get good at (financially speaking)!

Focus

Focus will also be required to build depth. When drawing out diagrams of depth in an organization, everything looks neat and tidy. But it won't feel that way as you learn to drive depth. That is because you are not constructing an organization of *diagrams*, you are constructing an organization of *people*. And that's where everything gets interesting. People are wonderful and frustrating all at the same time. They are predictable and unpredictable. They are hot and cold, rude and polite, mature and immature, ambitious (we like the word, "hungry" better) and lazy. And all those conflicts can exist within just one person!

It is up to you to stay focused on the objective of building a deep organization, even when the apparent complexity of multiple people with differing personalities and levels of interest become involved in your business. In one way, you have to make a connection with people and love them for being the special individuals they are. In another way, you must stay focused on moving the bottom of your organization deeper, no matter what.

Developing People Skills

We cannot, in any way, overemphasize this point: the ability to deal successfully with people will be absolutely required in order to build depth. As Robert Kiyosaki wrote, **"Your success or failure as an entrepreneur depends a lot on your people skills.** If you have strong people skills, your business will grow. If you have poor people skills, your business will suffer." We believe this to be exactly true in our business as well. That is the reason there is so much emphasis on developing people skills and personal growth in the Team's training system. Four of our "Top 5" books are aimed directly at helping the reader develop better people skills. These four books are, *How to Win Friends and Influence People*, by Dale Carnegie, *How I Raised Myself from Failure to Success* by Frank Bettger, *How to Have Confidence and Power in*

Dealing with People by Les Giblin, and *Personality Plus* by Florence Littauer.

Whenever you hear a business owner talking about his team, saying, "I can't get these people to . . . ," or "The people on my team won't . . . ," or "Why won't they . . . ?" it is a good indication that there may be a lack of people skills between the business owner and his team. Our experience is that people generally have a higher opinion of themselves in the area of people skills than the facts will actually allow. As one saying goes, "Reality and self-assessment are often very far apart."

Ability to deal with people is key. Even the very best among us should continue to study and improve. When it comes to effectively dealing with people, we never "arrive." We are always on the journey. With the Team training system, we know that journey will be in the positive direction. Sadly, with what the world generally feeds people, the journey is actually backwards. This is yet another reason why the CD's of the Week and Book of the Month programs are so critical. We must unlearn the bad habits with which we came into the business, and overcome the daily challenges that face us all at the same time.

Do we really listen to people? Are we really good at making friends? Are we able to overcome shyness and self-consciousness and reach out to others? Can we remember names and important details about people? Do we truly care about others? Are we unselfish and interested in serving other people? These questions and others ought to be our constant test to see how we are doing in the area of developing people skills. Growing personally in this area will be required to grow a big business, but it will also bring rewards in every area of your life. Get committed to improving your people skills, no matter how good they may already be. Depth in your organization depends on it!

Don't Hand Off Responsibility

To build depth in an organization, you will have to do it yourself. Team Approach is one thing, but ultimately, as we discussed before, "If it's to be, it's up to me." That is the only attitude that will result in a business that continually grows deeper and deeper. For depth to happen, you must take full responsibility yourself for making it grow.

Too many times we've seen people get involved in building depth in their organization and make one of two key mistakes. First, they expect their up-line leader to build it for them. "When are you going to do more to help me? When are you going to drive depth under me? How deep did you make it grow this week?" are all questions that people suffering from this mistake will ask. The other mistake is to think that someone below you in your organization will take over the building of depth for you. We call this "handing off of leadership responsibility." "Oh, I've got Bob and Mary in that group. They're going to go Diamond. So I'll just counsel them and encourage them," is the kind of thing said or thought by those suffering from this mistake.

Here is the best way to avoid either of these mistakes: never assume anyone else will ever do anything. **Take responsibility to do it yourself.** If someone else contributes, great, all the better. If not, no big deal, you were going to do it anyway. Besides, the people in your organization will copy the example they see from you. If you "expect" your up-line to build your business for you, others will expect the same coddling from you. If you "hand off" responsibility to someone in your group, they will do the same thing to people in their group. Leadership is not "handed" to anyone, it must be taken. When you are building the business properly, driving depth and building teams, people will spring up in your organization who crave leadership and responsibility. They will begin doing the right things, copying what they see their up-line doing, and moving the business forward on their own efforts. They will take responsibility for their actions, and results. It is when you start to have people like this in your organization that a transfer and sharing of leadership takes place. But it can never be "handed" or assigned to someone, it must be taken in this way, by force!

By avoiding either of these mistakes, you set a very visible example in your organization that others will copy. This will lead to faster growth, more harmonious teams, and more income!

There is another warning we should give here. One of the most common mistakes in the business is for people to get into something we call "management mode." This is a condition where someone begins *telling* others how to do the business, trying to *teach* them all that they know, instead of simply building it themselves. Often, the person doing this fakes himself out by thinking that this is *leadership* or *mentoring.* (For an in-depth explanation of the difference between management and leadership, see our book, *Launching the Leadership Revolution.*) Management mode is as far from leadership or mentoring as one could get! We can never mentor someone when we are new. Also, **we can never mentor someone when we don't have significant success and experience ourselves.** And, we can never mentor someone else if we are not being mentored, in turn. Finally, we can never mentor or teach someone to do something that we aren't doing ourselves! Until you have significant (and we mean significant) success and experience in the business, your responsibility for the grooming and leading of your people is the following:

1. Love your people
2. Work more than they do
3. Point to the training system, *not* to your own teaching!

Being Creative but Not Inventive

Over time, you will develop your own style within the framework of the pattern. There will always be room for you to be yourself and express your own personal style, to a degree, of course. But don't forget, the pattern is *proven.* Become inventive at your own peril. Following the pattern as it is, and mastering each step, will allow you to show the plan, get to the next person, show the plan a level deeper, and develop massive depth in your organization. Changing things, even a little, can take you off course. When you are just starting out, or when your group is small, this might not seem like such a big deal. But over time, being a little off course can take you way off.

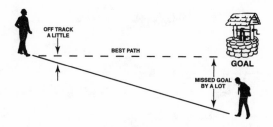

Also, as we explained above, being too inventive gets copied by your organization and can quickly lead to a mess. You'll have people everywhere thinking their little tweaks are the greatest inventions in the world; and at best, nothing will get accomplished, because chaos cannot build a community, only a mob. At worst, your business will resemble a mob and become unruly and destructive. We don't mean this literally, of course, but figuratively we've seen it happen. So stay within the proven techniques of the pattern. Get as creative as you want, in terms of creating a team, creating depth, creating new relationships, and creating massive product flow. But avoid getting inventive.

Personal Story

Names: Mark and Anna Huber
Former Occupations: Mechanical Engineer; Cosmetologist

I grew up in a great home in which my parents sacrificed and did their very best to provide for my three brothers and me. The refrigerator would go from full to empty in about 2 days - and my parents would find a way to fill it again (even if it was only with cheap beef stew and leftover lasagna). We were always encouraged to be active, adventurous and in so many words "to chase our dreams." Growing up with little money and in a factory town, my options, back then, seemed very limited.   Who knows where so many small decisions, or thin threads, over the course of one's life will lead? My decisions were leading me to follow what many other young American boys in peacetime are led to do: go to school, get good grades, get a good job (with benefits), raise a family and work to help your children have an even greater life than you had. My path was set - even though it felt like I was making my way through some foggy landscape with no well-defined destination.

During all of this, my parents did many wonderful things over the course of my life - opening doors and financing opportunities for us boys. However, little did my father know, he set up one of the most important little "thin threads" of my life - a short meeting between his 17 year old son and the most ambitious young man he could find.   That young man was Chris Brady, my father's supervisor at the time. This meeting was the thin thread that led to a faint recollection outside our company fueling station six years later – eventually leading to our 'second meeting' – and then a great business partnership.

Between these six years, I had been experiencing more of the world. I was expanding my dreams through study and occasional travel in college. On weekends I loved to listen to musicians sing about far away tropical paradises and relaxing days. Not long after, my dreams were injected with a type of "jet-fuel" when I took my senior trip - a cruise to the southern Caribbean! We snorkeled

162

in Granada and drank from fresh coconuts in Caracas, Venezuela. We snapped photos of each other with macaws perched on our head and out-stretched arms. Then, we sat in our beach chairs, feeling the sand between our toes, and watched a young couple with their two children jump off of a 50 ft. catamaran yacht they had just beached and walk to the nearby tiki-restaurant for lunch. "That's what I want when I become a success!" I thought to myself.

Another trip that fueled my dreams was my first trip with my wife to the Atlantis Resort in Paradise Island, Bahamas. We ate fresh grilled lobster next to the ocean. We splashed down water-slides and let our cares melt away under a waterfall. If our cares started to come back, they soon left after a nap in a hammock on Blue Lagoon Island. I was hooked! These images would be burned into my mind forever. This lifestyle had to become a part of wher-ever my life's path would take me.

When Chris and I sat down (for the second time), I was hungry (more like starving) for an opportunity that would lead me to make my newfound visions a reality. The only problem was that I was not really sure if I was the type of person that could succeed as an entrepreneur. My simple logic that kept me involved was that (1) I knew Chris was going to succeed at this, and (2) he said he would help me. That was all I needed to begin my journey. So we start-ed working on the biggest project I had ever really faced – myself. It took some time and a many hours of audio material to eventual-ly realize that the project was *me* - and the product of my efforts in business would inevitability produce a better me! (Then the money came in as a by-product of personal growth *plus* hard work). I did the best I could to follow exactly what Chris demon-strated and what was taught in the educational system he inces-santly kept promoting to me. I can still hear the sayings from early audio recordings that kept me in the action-mode through thick and thin: *"One good victory erases all past failures!"*, *"God honors commitment"* and, *"If I stay tough, I'll make it."*

After a lot of learning, stretching, and hard work, we were able to accomplish some wonderful victories along the way. We have not arrived by any means, but some of the blessings along the jour-ney thus far have been miraculous! I was able to travel more to the places of my dreams with my family, the Brady's, the Woodward's, and many other friends I made along the way. I was able to relieve the financial pressure that used to gnaw at me daily. I was able to replace my W-2 income at a very young age and be a full-time at-home father and husband. I was able to find clarity of purpose in what used to be fog. But most of all, I continue on this amazing personal growth journey that I hope and pray everybody gets a chance to experience.

I write these words as much to myself as to the reader: *"Sailboats are safe in the harbor, but were not made for the harbor."* I will always encourage as many people as I can to chase their dreams through a journey of personal growth and serving others with a business vehicle that has it all - the Team.

May God bless your journeys!

"Would the boy you were be proud of the man you are?"
- Anonymous

"We make a living by what we get. But we make a life by what we give."
- Winston Churchill

"Mastery is not something that strikes in an instant, like a thunderbolt, but a gathering power that moves steadily through time, like weather."
- John Champlin Gardner

"People forget how fast you did a job, but they remember how well you did it."
- Howard N. Newton

"I would rather take a thousand 'No's' than one 'I told you so!'"
- Orrin Woodward

Name: DETAIL DAN

Quote: "I just have a few more
questions. Suppose I sponsered
my cousin in the Virgin Islands,
and then he moved to Malta
and married an Italian. Would
his bonus checks convert to
lira, euros or dollars? And
would that change his PV/BV
ratio, and if so by how much?"

Chapter 9

Results
Conquer, Fortify, Domesticate

Being in business is not about being in "busyness," it is about getting things done. For a business owner, being busy doesn't make you successful, it only makes you tired! This is where becoming an entrepreneur can differ from a life in the corporate world. Many times as an employee, what is rewarded is seniority, attitude, one's relationship with the boss, the number of hours worked regardless off their effectiveness, and other factors that may or may not have anything to do with what an individual is actually accomplishing.

For entrepreneurs it is different. Looking the part, playing the games, and "talking the talk" will get you nowhere in the real world of owning your own business. To *make it*, you have to *make it happen*. You have to hold yourself accountable for results. The best way to keep yourself on track, honest about your performance, and improving all the time is by properly measuring your performance. No sport would be interesting to watch or play if the participants didn't have a scoreboard to know how they were doing. As a matter of fact, some have theorized that sports are such a popular entertainment for so many people exactly because immediate feedback is provided regarding how a team or individual is performing. Such is the life of an entrepreneur, also.

The way to understand your business properly is to know that you must learn to *lead people*, and *manage the numbers*. It is like breathing. You don't *only* breath in, and you don't *only* breath out. You must do *both*. In business, you must learn to become adept at both managing the numbers *and* leading the people. This chapter will focus on managing the numbers.

Conquer, Fortify, Domesticate

Throughout history there have been battles all over the face of the globe. In times past (and sometimes still today), much of the conflict was over territory. One ruler wanted the land that another ruler possessed. Ultimately, this conflict would lead to war, and armies would take to the field. In such a situation, the first aim of an army was to *conquer* new territory by taking it form the opposing army. Next, once an area had been overtaken and the enemy driven off, the victorious army would *fortify* that area, or secure their position. This would be accomplished by digging into the earth, erecting breastworks and redoubts, and building barricades or forts to keep the enemy from re-taking the territory. After a while, once the "coast was clear" and the enemy were safely repulsed from the territory, the area could then be *domesticated*. Settlers would be brought in to till the soil, women and children would come to live with their conquering heroes, and new towns and villages would be built.

Thankfully, the Team business does not require us to raise arms against an enemy. But it is a lot like a battle in that we have to *conquer* new territory in terms of growing our businesses bigger, *fortify* it by making it secure and long-lasting, and *domesticate* it by moving products. These three steps are a good reminder of the order of attack when building our organizations, as well as the proper measurements to consider when checking our progress and assessing the strength of our teams.

It is always a temptation to focus upon too many things in the business. People can run off in all directions doing this or that. But as we have said before, the most successful business owners always subscribe to the "what's important next" theory of doing things. They know that there are always many *good* things to do, but only one or two *great* things to do. Focusing on doing the great things at the expense of the good things is called prioritization. It is the proper prioritization of the business that the illustration of *conquer, fortify, domesticate* is designed to teach.

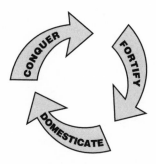

Incidentally, we could also re-label this diagram as Product, Process, Program.

Further, as we have been discussing, we could also refer to this concept as Information, Progress, and Income.

Finally, we could re-label this one final way, calling these steps Healthy, Wealthy, and Wise.

These labels are simply meant to provide helpful markers on the concepts that are central to building a community of people through which products and services flow. For the purpose of this chapter, we will continue to refer to these concepts using the Conquer, Fortify, Domesticate labels.

Conquer

The first priority in the business is one of conquering new territory. This involves showing the plan to new people. There are very few things that could be considered more important or more productive in the building of your business. Then, as we've already discussed, your whole goal is to get them involved in the training system. One of the best ways to measure how you are doing at this is to keep track of the number of seminar tickets that have been sold into your organization. This is called your Ticket Count. One of the best indicators of how much "territory" your business is conquering is the number of people you have attending seminars (or major functions, whichever happen to be occurring at the time).

When considering the "what's important next" principle, showing plans and moving tickets is definitely your starting point. Understand also, that as we discussed before, showing the plan is what leads the prospective new business owner to attend an Open Meeting. It is usually at an Open Meeting someone becomes convinced to attend a seminar. **So the strategy is to show a lot of plans, get everyone to the next Open Meeting, and then get them to the seminar.** (However, if you are showing them the plan and there is a seminar coming up without an opportunity to get them to an Open Meeting first, by all means, do so.)

You may also notice here why it is so important to involve as many business owners as possible in the Standing Order Ticket system. This way, they will automatically get their tickets each month. You can then invest your time in moving tickets to *new* people, therefore conquering new territory, and not having to re-conquer old territory over and over again.

Obviously, though, you will have no one to move tickets to if you haven't gained new territory. This can only be accomplished through building depth. The Conquer step, then, is really Depth and Power Player (both to be discussed below). This sets up the ticket counts.

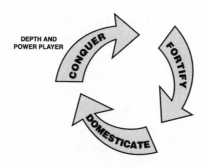

Odometer and Speedometer

When it comes to measuring your business, there are really two categories that you should be tracking. One can be called an Odometer measurement. An odometer on a car tells you how many total miles the vehicle has traveled. An odometer measurement of your business tells you how big it is. It basically measures the size of your team. However, an Odometer gives no indication as to the speed of your business, so another gauge is required, that of the Speedometer. A speedometer, obviously, tells you how fast the vehicle is traveling. Likewise in our business, you will be very interested to know and measure the speed of growth of your team.

When it comes to the principles of monitoring your business, these are the two main categories at which you will be looking: the size of your business and the speed of your business.

Depth

The natural state of the business is growth, just like a healthy child. It is not "holding your own" or "treading water." A key measurement you should be using to track the health and progress of your business is the magnitude and the pace at which the depth is happening in each of your organizations. When we talk about speedometer readings, this is a prime example. How many levels deeper is your business growing each month at the bottom of each of your organizations or legs?

Depth is a great concept, and it is our major strategic weapon, but it must be employed properly, and that means quickly. There is a pace to success, and it must be high enough to generate excitement and belief up through the organization. If depth grows too slowly, people can start to doubt the business and worse, their own ability to build it. But if depth grows quickly, people will get energized, confident, and active.

So keep track of the levels of depth you develop on a monthly basis. Counsel with your up-line to determine the appropriate levels of depth per month for which you should be aiming. Then make sure you are on pace. Make sure you are aiming at Power Player and accomplishing it in a fast enough amount of time. (The best business builders set a goal for accomplishing Power Player each month.) Remember, momentum is your best friend in this business. Go after it!

The number of levels in depth of your business is an *odometer* reading. It tells how big your business is. The pace at which your depth is progressing is a *speedometer* reading. It tells how fast your business is growing. Monitor both of these aspects of depth to get a clear picture.

Power Player Measurements

Now that we understand the theory and specifics of building depth, it is time to go back to the Power Player Program. And

172

remember, accomplishing or "going" Power Player tells you if you are building the business properly. You may recall that the Power Player Program encompasses three main components of building the Team business: theory, activity, and results. The particular results to measure in the Power Player Program are the *depth built in each of two organizations.*

To accomplish Power Player and receive the recognition and prestige that go along with it, (not to mention the business growth that results from its accomplishment), one must build one organization (sometimes called a "leg") ten levels deep, and a second organization five levels deep. Additionally, the ten deep leg must have a minimum of four business owners who have elected to subscribe to the "system" of CD's of the Week and Book of the Month. This must also be the case in the second organization to the tune of a minimum of two people subscribing. See the diagram below.

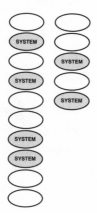

The other part of the Power Player requirement is 150 PV minimal volume of products generated through your particular business number, not including that volume generated by other business partners in your organization. This volume can include products you have purchased to use yourself, as well as those you have retailed to customers (known as clients). The generating of product volume will be explained in more depth a little later in this chapter. At this point, it should be noted that the Power Player Program requires a business owner to generate 150 PV per month.

Finally, a Power Player has at least ten people at Team seminars across the country that month. This is known as "Team 10," and includes you and your spouse.

When the theory and activity requirements of Power Player have consistently been filled, and the results are accomplished, then immediately one is recognized as a Power Player! The chart below summarizes the requirements for Theory, Activity, and Results for accomplishing the Power Player level.

THEORY	ACTIVITY	RESULTS
• Standing order CD's • Book of the month • Top 50 CD set • Standing order seminar ticket(s) • Attend all weekly meetings • Attend Men's/Ladies Leadership meetings • Subscribe to www.the-team.biz • Subscribe to voicemail system	• Show at least 15 plans a month. The plans can be shown to people from your list and/or to people from the lists of IBO's in depth • Generate 150 points (PV) per month • Participate in the DOT1/STEP Program	• Help one team in your business go at least 10 new levels in depth with at least 4 of the new IBO's on the training system • Help a second team in your business go at least 5 new levels in depth with at least 2 of the new IBO's on the training system • Have 10 people, including you and your spouse, if applicable, attending local seminars

Your First Sixty Days

You only have one chance to get started properly in the business. The right way to do that is to make Power Player your focus from day one. Remember, people with a specific goal will accomplish far more than those with no clear target.

In your first thirty days, you should focus entirely on building your *first team*: that body of people who will be positioned "below" you in the organization. This is called your "apprenticeship team" or "apprenticeship leg." Rotate the Five Step Pattern and help your up-line build depth. Combine efforts with your up-line to develop that first group at least ten levels deep in the first month. Then, you will want to fortify that new team by placing at least four of them "on system" as we just described.

In your second thirty days, ideally, you should shift your focus to your "second team" or "second leg." Create this new team to be at least five levels deep with two of the new business owners "on system." With that accomplished, you've satisfied the major portion of the results required to qualify as a Power Player! It's that straight forward!

At this point, it may be helpful to answer in advance a frequently asked question: "At what point is it appropriate for one to start his or her second leg?" There are several parts to this answer. First, it is your business, and you can build it any way that you wish. But what we strongly recommend is that you ascribe to the following proven checklist before venturing out into your second leg:

1. Be "on system" yourself.
2. Have at least four business owners underneath you "on system" in your first leg.
3. Replace yourself in that first leg; in other words, bring into the business at least one new business owner at your level of commitment and excitement, or above.

Once accomplishing Power Player, however, it is not time to take a rest. The worst thing in the world you can do after a major accomplishment is to take a rest. Why? Because that kills all the momentum you've developed. Feel free to celebrate for a moment; after all, you've earned it. But quickly get back to work on the path toward your dreams. The proper thing to do is keep the pace going and qualify for Power Player again, which effectively would be what we call a Double Power Player. Now to do that, it doesn't mean you have to do twice the amount of monthly Theory or Activity, but it does mean that you have to achieve twice the amount of *Results*. So a Double Power Player would be a business owner who achieved the monthly Theory and Activity requirements while building a leg twenty deep with a minimum of eight business owners subscribing to the system and a second leg ten deep with a minimum of four business owners subscribing to the system. The volume requirement of 150 PV stays as it is.

Feel free also to continue the momentum even further and beyond Double Power Player. The business owners who have accomplished these awesome levels obviously have had the fastest growing businesses nation-wide.

Fortify

The *next* most important thing to do is to fortify the new territory you have gained. This means strengthening your new business and making it more secure. This is done by involving your organization in the informational training system consisting of books, CD's, DVD's, pamphlets, etc. It will also start them on a path toward personal growth and learning that is the prerequisite to success in the Information Age. Additionally, it will help "beat back" the daily doses of negative people receive out there in the world.

So the fortify step is really a measure of how well you have *systematized* your team. The best way to do this, of course, is to make sure you have systematized yourself, first. Become a tool expert. Become a tool dispenser. Make the system work for you by having its items on hand and leveraging them liberally. Spreading tools around society is a lot like planting seeds for a future harvest. Want a bigger business? Plant more tools! Understanding this, the new diagram would look like this:

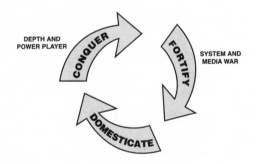

DEPTH AND POWER PLAYER — CONQUER — FORTIFY — SYSTEM AND MEDIA WAR — DOMESTICATE

<u>Standing Order Tools</u>

If fortifying your business is important, then it follows that the number of business owners on your team who are subscribing to the training system is a good measurement of results. Your System Count (the number of CD's of the Week and Books of the Months subscribed to by your organization) is one of the business's biggest and best indicators. This is because the weekly and monthly tool subscriptions have been proven to be critical to the ongoing training of an organization. The CD's of the Week and the Books of the Month go out to the entire subscribing organization, all over the hemisphere, and give everybody the same information at the same time. In this Information Age in which we live, having access to the correct information on a timely basis has never been so important. Having that information pure and timely, and most importantly, duplicatable, is fertilizer to the growth of your business. On the Team, we have never had anyone achieve any significant level of product flow, organization size, or growth without the use of the ongoing training program subscriptions. While they are optional, they have proven to be one of the best measures of how well an organization is being trained, is maintaining its attitude, and is moving forward.

Standing Order Tools are primarily an odometer reading that tells you the size of your organization, but by making comparisons to previous weeks, you can get a feel for the speedometer side of the business, too. You should aim for an increase in your standing order tool count every week.

Special Order Tools

We have been talking about different ways to measure and monitor your business in order to track your performance and stay on target toward your goals and dreams. However, there is one aspect to each of these measurements that they all have in common: they can only indicate what is actually happening in your business at that time. In other words, they have only limited *predictive* value as to what will happen in your business in the future.

To explain, let's consider the trading of stocks, for instance, in which there are two schools of thought as to the best way to go about it. The first method, called *fundamental* stock trading, focuses on exactly that, the fundamentals of a particular business. How is that business performing? How talented is the management team? What do their financials look like? And other questions like these are considered. A second method, called *technical* trading, focuses on something entirely different. For every company with a publicly traded stock, there is a chart that shows the history of activity regarding that stock. Actually, there are many charts. These charts show the fluctuation of price over time. They also show price versus the volume of shares traded, the size of blocks traded at a time, etc. According to technical traders, it is possible to determine the quality of an investment merely by reading the charts properly. A valuable piece of information to have would be the predictive value of whether or not the price of a stock were about to go up or down. A feature on a chart that gives such a prediction is called a *leading indicator*. It indicates what will happen *before* it actually does.

Special order tools are the best leading indicator in our business. *Special order tools* are training aids and support materials that are ordered above and beyond anything that is subscribed to on the "standing order" program. (For instance, CD's of the Week and Book of the Month are not special order tools, they are standing order tools.) Almost without exception, whenever an organization has a high hunger level for special order tools, the group is about to encounter explosive growth. This is due to several reasons.

First of all, tools are the secret to expanding the business because they are the purest form of teaching available. The speaker on a CD giving a talk about a certain topic gives it the exact same way every time! He or she also does the exact same talk for everybody and anybody who listens to it anywhere in the world. This is the purest form of duplication available, because everybody gets the same message. It can also be listened to repeatedly, heightening the understanding and education of the listener. The same, obviously, can be said for books.

Secondly, when tools are moving through an organization it is proof that the leader or leaders in that group are committed to growing their business. Nobody invests in tools to hand out to people unless he or she is planning on showing the plan to some people to which the tools can be handed! For that reason, when tools are flowing, you can rest assured that there are about to be a lot of plans shown in that group. And remember, this business grows based on the number of exposures to new people per unit of time.

Thirdly, tools broaden the relatability of the person showing the plan. Let's face it, we each have a special personality all our own. That fact can be both good and bad! Try as we might, with all the people skills we can learn, we are just not going to relate to everybody. That's where the tools come in. The prospect may not have related to you too well during the plan, but chances are high that he or she will relate to somebody they will hear on a CD. In this way, it broadens our relatability and increases our chances of connecting the right people to the business.

Finally, tools are so important to your business, because they carry the truth. The books, CD's and pamphlets focus on helping people unlearn the wrong teaching some have absorbed all of their lives and help them to finally learn the right stuff. It is common for us to hear new people say things like, "Where has this information been all my life?" "Why didn't they teach me this stuff in school?" "If I'd have only known about you guys sooner!" As the saying goes, "Truth is sweet to the ears." People know the truth when they hear it, especially those who have been hungering for it.

For these reasons, make sure you have an appropriate stock of extra tools to provide to people. And everywhere you go, **promote tools like seeds of a future harvest.** You can't reap if you don't sow.

Sometimes, at this point, people inquire as to the profits that may be made on the sale of tools in the business. In our book, *Leading the Consumer Rebellion*, which gives an overall introduction to the Team business, we explained the concept of profit sharing that is available for the training side of the business. The best way to understand this is to consider that there are four businesses within the business that are all complementary to each other: a product business (by far the largest revenue), tools business, speaking business, and an events business. Full profit sharing is conducted for each of these businesses across the board. Anyone can make more than anyone else. Each one of these businesses is available to every business owner, based upon performance. (Most rewards begin at or near the Platinum level.) There are no "grandfathered" incomes, no reward for "seniority," but just plain old reward for performance, just as it should be. As Plato and

Aristotle of old charged students to attend their academies, and as these academies lived or died based on the quality of information shared (as determined by their "customers," the students), so too runs the Team training system. Purchases are voluntary, and those who disseminate the information the best, and do the best job helping their team utilize the information to grow and succeed, will stand to profit the most from their efforts.

The Media War

The Information Age has changed all the rules. Those with the correct information win. Those with wrong information lose. It doesn't matter how old you are, how much experience you have, or how long you have been with your employer. When the rules change, they change for *everybody*. Adapt to the new rules, or get left behind.

The new rules say that information is king. Success will depend on getting the *correct* information and acting upon it. That is exactly what the Team's system of training materials and meetings is designed to do. How do we know our system contains the "right" information? Because the information we applied has worked for us and many others, and in various areas of our lives. We know we are nothing special. We had tried our hardest acting upon Industrial Age advice in an Industrial Age system with Industrial Age companies. What we got were mediocre results.

We had an inferior set of operating principles, or inferior *information*. Then, someone connected us to mentors who actually had succeeded financially and understood the rules of the new economy. We simply started listening, and then applied our efforts in that direction. It worked. We are the same guys, but experienced vastly different results. *That's* the value of the information. *That's* the value of learning the truth about business, finance, people, personal growth, entrepreneurship, and the Information Age. And *that's* what our training system does.

Each one of us every day receives hundreds of messages from the world about how to live, what to wear, how to act, what to buy, and what our values should be. We are bombarded by television, newspaper, radio, music, e-mail, junk mail, junk e-mail, pop-ups, spam, news, magazines, and association with people we may or may not choose to spend so much time with (fellow employees, for example). This is junk food for junk thinking. Learning proper thinking, learning *wealth-thinking*, will involve the undoing and the "beating back" of some of these destructive inputs. That's what the Team's training system does. And as you can see, it becomes a war of information. It becomes a *Media War*.

We have chosen to introduce this concept here because how well you do in waging the Media War will really be *the* indicator of how well you are building your business. The Team business doesn't compete with other word-of-mouth marketing companies. We don't compete with other sales organizations. We don't compete with other businesses, at all. What we compete with is the message of mediocrity that the world continues to sell us: a message that says we *can't* make it big; we *don't* deserve success; that playing small is somehow noble; that success is for "somebody else," and that doing "pretty good" is good enough. As author Bill Perkins wrote, "No weapon . . . has been more effective than the barrage of propaganda that hammers away at our thinking and convinces us we're not warriors. It urges us to kick back and watch the world pass by like a parade. Such passivity reeks of danger."

Well, the Team stands directly opposed to such passivity. We know that every person has the seeds of greatness inside of them, and we use our tools, our training system, to water and nurture those seeds. We have seen people the world had left behind join our business and thrive through the information we gave them. We have seen others who were hooked on status and on "looking good," actually learn to *truly* do well in life. We have seen people struggling in the grip of addictions break free and begin to regain control and dignity because of the inspiration they received from our training system. Now don't get us wrong, we are not taking credit for this. We don't have all the answers. But we know the power of the truth. We have seen it first hand, in our own lives and in the lives of others, and we are committed to spreading it as far as we possibly can.

Do you want to really know how well your business is doing? Do you want an accurate unit of measure? Take a look at how well the people who have chosen to join your business with you are doing. Have you done all that you can to get the truth into their hands? Have you seen them change because of something they heard on a CD or read in a book? Have you had people open up with you and share challenges because they want to grow and improve? Have you seen negative attitudes turn into positive attitudes? Have you seen husbands start treating their wives better? Have you seen wives treating their husbands better? Have you seen people's hearts grow warmer and warmer? As you build your business, look for those types of things in the lives of the people who enter your organization. *That's* the heart of success in this business. Actually, that's the heart of success in *life*. **Make your ultimate measure of success in the business the number of people you have helped along the way. Oh yeah, and as a result, you'll make some money, too.**

Domesticate

Domesticating your business means making sure that you develop product flow through the organization you have created. This is the step where you help people learn how to move products.

There are several ways in which products flow. One is to sell to retail customers. Another is for business owners to take advantage of the DOT1/STEP Program. In short, products flow three ways:

1. Products handed out as advertisements
2. Purchases made by clients
3. Personal consumption by business owners (DOT1/STEP)

It is important to note again, at this point, that your organization will duplicate the example they see in you. If you expect products to move through your organization, be sure to move them and consume them yourself!

DOT1/STEP Program

We have already talked about the DOT1/STEP Program, but the Ditto On the 1st and the Sip Twice, Eat and Profit portion of our business is an enormous part of your business building strategy. When discussing results in your business and how to track it properly, we must ultimately get down to talking about *product flow*. After all, we build communities for the purpose of moving products and services and receiving the profits from those sales. And, by far, the best way we have ever encountered for moving products through our communities is the DOT1/STEP Program.

First of all, the new people who sign up get their starter pack of sample products. Although it is very difficult for most new people to do, they should refrain from eating and drinking all of these initial products themselves. The purpose of the original starter pack is to provide sample products that may be handed out as they begin to expose their business to potential new business owners.

Secondly, the first actual Ditto order to the new business owner hits on the first of the month following their signup. *These* products are intended for the new business owner's personal consumption, retail sales, or for additional product samples and advertising.

What to look for in terms of measuring performance in your business is the number of *single, unmarried* business owners who have at least 50PV in Ditto on the 1st of the month orders of STEP products on a monthly basis. Married business owners should have at least 100PV in Ditto on the 1st of the month orders of STEP products on a monthly basis. Business owners who adhere to these recommended guidelines will be invited to special meetings and will qualify for special recognitions. Tracking the number of such qualifiers lets you know how well the basic building block of moving products is duplicating in your group. If you have new signups, but they aren't getting involved with the DOT1/STEP program, somebody needs to be educated on the principles of duplication and "what's in it for them." Remember, it's the principle of *duplication* that leads to massive businesses. Discretion and divergence don't. Monitor your DOT1/STEP qualifiers to check your team's ability in this area.

Perhaps at this point it may be helpful to relate a little story about one of the world's most successful professional athletes, because most people don't understand what it means to be "under contract" to represent a certain product. They join the business and don't necessarily understand that, just like a high-profile professional athlete, they too now have a contract with a manufacturer that pays them for loyalty and increased product usage. The athlete to which we refer is Michael Jordan. In his book, *Driven From Within*, Jordan's best friend relates a story that illustrates the loyalty and commitment that not only propelled Jordan to the top of the sporting world, but to the top of the product endorsement world, as well. According to Fred Whitfield,

"Michael's whole being is about loyalty and winning. He really feels like you can't ride the fence. You have got to be loyal to what you believe in, and then always believe you're going to win. That's probably what I have learned from him over all these years.

I was really close to Ralph Sampson. Ralph had a big Puma contract coming out of the University of Virginia. He was Puma's man. When I would go up to Boston with Ralph, we'd go to the Puma warehouse. I would do the same thing when I'd go out to Nike with Michael. They'd say, 'Whatever you want, pick it out and we'll ship it to you.' I had my closet separated out, half Puma, half Nike. I had 25 or 30 pairs of Pumas . . . . Then I had all my Air Jordans, Nike stuff.

Michael comes to my apartment in Greensboro one time. We're getting ready to go out, and he says, 'Man, it's kind of cold. Can I borrow one of your jackets?' I said, sure, go in my closet. He went in there and saw everything separated out. He's in there a little longer than necessary, and here he comes out of my room.

He's taken all my Puma stuff, brought it out into the living room and laid it on the floor. He goes into the kitchen, gets a butcher knife and literally cuts up everything. This was like his second or third year in the league. He literally took a butcher knife, and he's inside the suede shoes, ripping, cutting. When he's all done, he picks up every little scrap and walks it all down to the dumpster.

He says, 'Hey dude, call Howard tomorrow and tell him to replace all of this. But don't ever let me see you in anything other than Nike. You can't ride the fence.' From that day forward, I've never worn anything that wasn't Nike. That's the degree to which he believes.

If you walk into a room with Michael, the first thing he's going to do is look at you from head to toe. He's going to look at your feet."

We share this story in its entirety not because it shows how extreme Michael Jordan is, but because it shows how well he understands business. When it comes to loyalty, 99% loyalty is 100% *disloyalty*. Jordan understood that he was being paid to do a job. And he became the biggest "business" professional athlete the sporting world had yet seen, and set the standard for all athletes to follow.

Jordan understood that the master copy had to be worth copying. In our business, which runs on the concept of duplication, it should be equally important for us to be product loyal. Now don't get us wrong, we are certainly not promoting the idea that you should show up with tin snips and start cutting up your business partner's soda cans! But the principle of loyalty should be clear.

Set a strong example yourself, and measure the number of people loyal to their own products through the DOT1/STEP program to track your business's health.

By the way, it is also commendable to purchase and sell products from the more than one million other product offerings that we represent. This should be done only *beyond* conformance to the building block of DOT1/STEP, however. Remember, if you demonstrate the best, most duplicatable principle, it will be easier and more profitable for everyone in your business to follow that example.

Overall PV

Overall point value is obviously important, too. As you climb the performance bonus chart, this total is what you will compare to the chart to determine the amount of your monthly bonus check. It will also be the number you look at *per organization or leg* that you build within your team. This number can be obtained on the same website screen referred to above.

PERFORMANCE BONUS SCHEDULE

If Your Total Monthly PV is:	Your Performance Bonus is :
7,500 or more	25% of your BV
6,000	23%
4,000	21%
2,500	18%
1,500	15%
1,000	12%
600	9%
300	6%
100	3%

As we add these types of measurements of product flow to how we look at our business, we can see that we now have a complete circle.

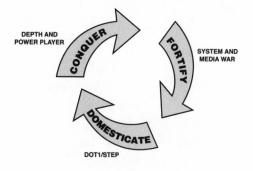

Summary

Knowing what to measure in the performance of your business will go a long way to staying on track and producing consistent, sustaining growth. Remember, the principle is to lead people and manage numbers.

Personal Story

Names: Jim and Delores Martin
Former Occupations: Master Plumber;
Wife/Mom (Domestic Engineer)

In the summer between 11th and 12th grade I was grounded for having low grades, when along came my cousin to my rescue. He offered to have me come to work with him as an apprentice plumber. I thought, "What a great idea. I'll be out of the house and be making money, too." That was the start of a fifteen year career.

I was never afraid of hard work, and when I graduated I took everyone's advice to go into plumbing and forget college. (My grades were never very high.) It was great. My income doubled after only nine months on the job. After just three years, I studied hard and passed the Journeymen's test on the first try. It was so gratifying to see how my hard work paid off. As a kid I always wanted to do something great. I thought this was going to be my ticket.

I started to buy toys galore, including a brand new truck, all on the assumption that my income would always keep growing. This was when I met Dolores, the girl of my dreams. We were married and started a family, and it seemed that everything for my life started to fall into place. I received my Masters in Plumbing and started to work harder everyday just to keep up with the lifestyle we had always dreamed of. At this time I branched out and started my own plumbing business on top of working for my current employer. I was under the impression that working harder and harder was the only answer.

The stress of self-employment started to pile up and I was seeing my family less and less. I would work all day for my employer, come home, eat dinner, and then go back out for my own business. At times I would call Dolores and tell her that there had to be more to life than this. I just didn't know of anything. Everything that I had hoped life would be started to slip away. Dolores and I started to grow further apart, and at times I wondered if the kids even knew who I was. "How could this happen," I often thought, "I'm doing what everyone told me to do."

That is when we were invited to a neighbor's house to see this business plan. I signed up the first night, with hopes that this was something that *Dolores* could do. I couldn't have been more wrong. She wanted nothing to do with it. Thankfully, the gentleman showing the plan left us with materiel to listen to and booked a time to get back together. After listening to the information and sitting back down with him I decided to attend an Open Meeting. That Tuesday night gave me so much insight into what I was doing wrong. It wasn't about working *harder*. I needed to start working *smarter*. I got fully involved with the training system and felt like a lead brick had been lifted off of me. The hope I once had for our future had returned!

The only hurdle I could see was getting Dolores on board. She agreed to attend a seminar with me and that night she too got a bigger picture of where the Team was headed. Now she too wanted to be apart of it. It was exciting to receive CD's every week and to actually listen to people that had already been across the mine field and were willing to teach us to get to the other side, too.

It challenged me when I noticed that there weren't a lot of construction workers on stage speaking yet. I took it upon myself to let the system work for me and everyone on my team. I started to listen to nine CD's a day, plugged into a mentor, and even learned to love reading. It was through the books that I discovered better ways to manage my income, learned people skills, gained leadership principles, and much more.

This has been way more then just a business to Dolores and me. It has been challenging at times, for sure, but how gratifying life has become now that we are tied into a vehicle that rewards performance like nothing else out there. After just two years in the business, I was able to flush (no pun intended) that plumbing career and start living life the way God intended: that is, living my *priorities* not my *obligations*.

Dolores and I are forever indebted to the Team for giving us a way to help others receive hope for their futures, also.

Pay it forward!

"You can't build a reputation on what you are going to do."
- Henry Ford

"You can spend your whole life any way you want to, but you can only spend it once."
- Dwight Thompson

"Life is not a dress rehearsal."
- Peter Daniels

"When you're green, you're growing. When you're ripe, you're not."
- Ray Kroc

"There is no more miserable human being than the one in whom nothing is habitual but indecision."
- William James

Name: FRAIDY-CAT FRED

Quote: "Oh, um, my list? I just can't seem to find it. It's not really done anyway. Besides, I really need to study that contacting script for a few more weeks, before I make any calls. "

Chapter 10

Business Ownership
The Principles

Now that we have surveyed the wealth of information available on how to build a community of people through which products and services flow, it is time to put it all together. There are many overarching principles, and a host of specifics, that are required to complete the package. In this chapter, we will focus on the principles, which will not only make all the steps we've discussed to this point easier to accomplish, they will also make them more fruitful.

Deny Yourself

One of the most important things to learn about becoming a business owner, whether in this business or any other, is to deny yourself. We live in an instant gratification world. Everybody wants things right now, and they want them perfect, and they want them to be easy. Unfortunately, none of that is reality, especially when talking about greatness and success. These things take time, and they take the application of self-discipline. As mathematician and philosopher Pythagoras said centuries ago, "Make self-control a habit."

It is okay to keep *good* things from yourself so that you can later earn *great* things. It is okay to do without for a little while. It is okay to go backwards to go forwards. And it is okay to be tough on yourself and allow yourself to struggle. You will never see a champion who babies him or herself, or has to give in to every whim and urge. Self-discipline, and the ability to give up in the short term so that you can obtain in the long term is not only a sign of maturity, it is a prerequisite to success and significance. It is also a choice. As a business owner, be sure to make that choice daily.

193

Be Consistent

As we discussed earlier in this book, little things lead to big things. But this is only true if those little things are done properly, and if they are done *consistently*. As author Alexander Lockhart wrote, "The success or failure of your life depends not so much on how hard you try, but the accumulation of your efforts, and whether you keep at it." For efforts to accumulate, they must be consistent.

In the business, it is common for someone to get really excited and begin taking the correct steps. Then suddenly, something pops up to distract them. Maybe a promotion comes up at work, or a family struggle occurs, or a new romance blooms, or football season starts, or the kids go back to school, or it's time to clip one's finger nails. We've seen it time and time again; someone gets off to a great start, they begin developing momentum in their learning and in their business, then they let the smallest thing knock them off course. One of our favorite quotes is this, "Most men fail because of broken focus." Focus is the secret weapon of a champion. Talent and effort can only bear fruit as a result of focus, and consistent focus at that. There is a legend that the great philosopher Aristotle was once asked by a passerby, "How do you get to Mount Olympus?" to which the great sage replied, "By ensuring that each step you take is in that direction." That's the meaning of consistency: ensure that each step is in that direction.

How does one stay consistent in the business? After all, knowing that one *should* stay consistent, and then actually *remaining* consistent are two different things. The answer lies in the power of our dreams to motivate us. The best way to stay consistent is to stay committed to your dream. Look at your dreams on a regular basis. In a previous book, *Launching a Leadership Revolution*, we went into depth on this idea in a section called *Dream building*. The basic concept is that you won't be properly driven to achieve greater results in your life until you familiarize yourself with what those results could be. This might involve going to look at new homes, or test driving a new car, or simply visualizing your last day at work. If we deny the power of our dreams, we deny one of the biggest sources of power within us, a power that can drive us to be consistent. Another way to stay consistent is to stay plugged into the training system. Listening to CD's on a regular basis, reading the books, and associating with other business owners who are excited about the business cannot help but to build consistency, also. Just realize this: consistency is one of your best friends. Treat him properly, and he will reward you accordingly.

Set the Example

Abraham Lincoln once said, "Example isn't the *main* thing in influencing other people, it's the *only* thing." While there are some that wouldn't take it quite that far, there can be no debating the importance of personal example in any enterprise. This is doubly true in the Team business. Our business is one of relationships with other people, and those people will look to you for a map on how to behave, conduct their own business, and respond to situations.

This surprises most people when they are new to the business. Perhaps they have lived their lives, earned their money, and spent their time in ways where they didn't have to face up to how they had affected other human beings. But *all* of us have an effect on others. And to build a strong business, we must be conscious of our example and make sure it is a good one, even if it is the first time we've ever had to do so. This is because the Team business builds on a concept called *duplication*, which we'll discuss in greater detail in a little while. For now, suffice it to say that duplication is the idea that the master will be copied, in all ways, good and bad. If you have a bad attitude, that attitude will duplicate down through your organization. Likewise with a good attitude. If you are short with people, or selfish, or lazy, or any other negative attitude, you will surely see signs of those attitudes showing up in your group. But if you are patient, selfless, energetic, and positive, you should see a group of people copying your example. Of course, we don't live in a perfect world. And the humorous saying that rings only too true goes as follows: "Your group will duplicate 100% of the things you do wrong, and only about 50% of the things you do right." For this reason, we'd better be extra careful with our personal example and make sure it is a good one!

Expect the Best Out of People

Any fool can find fault; it takes somebody special to find greatness. In order to build a big business, it becomes absolutely necessary that we see the good in other people. Some have called this "becoming a good-finder." Others have suggested the best way to do this is to "catch others in the act of doing something right." Whatever the recipe, it is important to understand the power you have in the lives of others when you hold them to a standard and expect them to live up to it.

This doesn't mean that you impose your iron-will on people. And it doesn't mean that they have to perform to satisfy your demands. What it involves is meeting people where they are, but expecting them to become the best they can be. It is the difference between mere friendship and something that heads in the direction of mentorship. A friend will allow you to be who you are. A mentor will expect you to become the best you can be.

Expecting the best out of someone could also mean that someone likes the way they see themselves when they look at themselves through *your* eyes. As we have said many times in the business, "Your people need to be able to see *their* victory in *your* eyes." Let's face it. People can go just about anywhere to get dumped on. They can hear negative and pessimism anywhere. But there are very few places, perhaps none, where they can go to be uplifted, encouraged, and believed in. We need to make sure that those joining the Team business know beyond a shadow of doubt that they have a person or group of people that believes in them, and expects the best they have to give.

It has been said that, "You will discover your true greatness as soon as you begin to *feel* and *see* yourself as a great person." The Team business is about finding people, identifying their greatness, and showing it to them continually until they begin to see it for themselves. People are the happiest when they live up to the highest expectations they have of themselves. Let's help them *raise*

196

those expectations, see those expectations, and *realize* those expectations.

Build Relationships

To hold people to highs standards and give them a true, higher picture of themselves, we must first develop a *relationship* with them. As the saying goes, "People don't care how much you know until they know how much you care." We have found no truer maxim when attempting to influence people.

As Tim Marks says, "If you want to help someone, *help them like you first.*" What Tim is driving at is that for a relationship to be built, one must become relatable and likeable to other people. This is the reason there is so much emphasis in the Team training system on people skills. We all come into the business deficient, to some degree, in this area. And no matter how good we become in dealing with people, we can and should always get better. Another Tim Marks statement says, "Activity minus people skills plus time equals frustration." You can do a lot of work, but without good interactions with people, it will be in vain.

There are those that are chronic over-talkers, while others are painfully shy. Some are too loud, brash, and boastful, while others have annoying mannerisms like interrupting or finishing people's sentences for them. We must all analyze ourselves just a little, and reduce our weaknesses while we focus most of our attention on enhancing our strengths. And we must also become good at overlooking those annoying tendencies in others.

An anonymous poem does a good job of succinctly summarizing some very important people skills:

> The six most important words:
> I admit I was wrong.
> The five most important words:
> You did a great job.
> The four most important words:
> What do you think?
> The three most important words:

Could you please . . .
The two most important words:
Thank you.
The one most important word:
We.

People skills open the door to relationships. But people skills are just that, *skills*. What has to happen in a relationship is something more, something deeper. There must be caring and sincerity. To build a relationship, we must really connect with the other person. We must find common ground, develop mutual respect, and offer a listening ear. We probably shouldn't resort to another poem so quickly, but we can't resist.

If I Knew You

If I knew you and you knew me;
If both of us could clearly see,
And with an inner sight divine,
The meaning of your heart and mine.
I'm sure that we should differ less;
And clasp our hands in friendliness;
Our thoughts would pleasantly agree,
If I knew you and you knew me.

If I knew you and you knew me,
As each one knows his own self, we
Could look each other in the face,
And see therein a truer grace.
Life has so many hidden woes,
So many thorns for every rose,
The "why" of things our hearts would see
If I know you and you knew me.

- N. Waterman

To build a relationship with someone is to drive at really *knowing* him or her. When that happens, they will give you permission to influence them, help them, and lead them. But nurture such relationships tenderly; they are among the most wonderful "things" on earth.

Before leaving this section, we want to emphasize that the building of relationship is perhaps the most important thing to learn in the entire business. Blow this one, and blow it all. Take this lightly, and your business will treat you lightly. Do poorly at this step, and *perfection* in rotating the pattern, listening to CD's, showing the plan, or whatever else, will produce mediocrity at best. On the other hand, get good at this step, and you can be sloppy at all the others and things will work out just fine!

Develop Character

There are really two types of abilities with people, both of which are important. The first is the ability to make a good first impression, what we have elsewhere in this book called relatability. The second is the ability to build deeper and more meaningful relationships with people as they become more familiar with you. For this second category, the pertinent question is: do people like you more or less as they get to know you better?

At the heart of this second kind of ability with people is the question of *character*. Are we who we say we are? Does our walk match our talk? Phonies will get exposed, sooner or later. As the saying goes, "Always tell the truth, then you won't have to keep track of everything you say." As Abraham Lincoln famously said, "You can fool all of the people some of the time, some of the people all of the time, but not all of the people all of the time."

People who lack character sometimes behave as if they think they are "getting away with it," that somehow others aren't picking up on their deceptions or dishonesty. But this is rarely the case. Lies only hold up for so long, and when they see the light of day, they normally burn through the trust in relationships in a hurry. Once trust is gone, the relationship is in dire jeopardy. Only time, forgiveness, maturity, repentance, personal change, and a host of other benevolences can rebuild what was destroyed.

It is far better to guard our character and build on it daily. As R.C. Samsel said, "Character is the foundation stone upon which one must build to win respect. Just as no worthy building can be erected on a weak foundation, so no lasting reputation worthy of respect can be built on a weak character. Without character, all effort to attain dignity is superficial, and the results are sure to be disappointing."

To build relationships, and build our businesses, we best build on a foundation of character. And that foundation is built brick by brick, one day at a time. Build wisely.

Choose Your Responses

When building a business with other people, we must develop the maturity to choose our responses to the little situations that will eventually come up from time to time. That ability to choose, based on our *emotional intelligence* and not our *emotional knee-jerk reaction*, will go a long way to developing relationships with others and demonstrating the depth of our character.

There will be occurrences and circumstances that will arise. There will be challenges. It seems like when dealing with people, there is always something amiss. Many times, our response to the problem is more important than the problem itself. If we have a tendency to "fly off the handle," "boil over," "pitch a fit," "lose our cool," "come unglued," "get our knickers in knots," "have our tail feathers ruffled," "hit the ceiling," "get our noses out of joint," "bite someone's head off," "give a piece of our mind," "grind our axe," "read them the riot act," "let them have it," "give them what they've got coming to them," "dress them down," "take the gloves off," "tell them a thing or two," "get a load off," "tell them where it's at," "lose control," "tell them where they can - " well, you get the idea, then we will damage relationships and our ability to influence others. A famous phrase says, "We are only as big as the smallest thing that upsets us."

Author Dave Balter wrote, "The way a company responds to negative word-of-mouth can create positive word-of-mouth.

According to a study by Glynn Mangold et al., half of all negative word-of-mouth comes from consumers who feel a sense of injustice about the way they are treated by a company when they have a problem, rather than by the shortcomings in the product or service itself. So, the way a company responds to negative . . . becomes an important part of the conversation, possibly the most important." If choosing a proper response is appropriate for a company, certainly it is important for an individual business owner choosing to build a big business, too. We must learn to choose our responses, and to choose well.

How do we do this? Firstly by realizing that in the Team business, there really are no emergencies. Nothing is *that* urgent that it's worth "blowing our stack," or "throwing down with someone," or, well, never mind (sometimes we just can't help it!) Also, it will be helpful to realize that when people do things that bring us to anger, they probably didn't do it on purpose. It is extremely doubtful that someone would wake up one morning and think, "You know, I think I'll screw up so-and-so's day today. I know just how to hurt his feelings!" Instead, we should be quick to give someone the benefit of the doubt, and slow to give them the wrath of our shout. Most circumstances turn out to be misunderstandings. If we choose an appropriate, controlled, loving, patient response to the things that occur, we will leave the door open to actually solving the problems at hand.

Give More Than Is Expected

There is a story told of a builder whose son wanted to enter the trade with him. To begin, the father allotted $200,000 to the son for the purpose of constructing his first house. Upon sale of the home on the open market, father and son would split the proceeds. By all accounts, this was a great deal for the son. Unfortunately, the son's honor was not in line with the father's generosity. Throughout the project, the son cut corners and cheapened the quality of the house in order to make secret profits. By the end of the project, more than $50,000 had been "shaved" in this way from the construction cost of the home. Most of these economies were taken from the structure and foundation of the building where inspectors and generous fathers would not notice. As the project neared completion, the father burst out with happy news: the home was to be a gift to the son! He could keep the house for his own!

Many people go through life giving less than their best. They cut corners and take the easy way out, ignoring the maxim that "if there's a job worth doing, it's worth doing right." There seems to be a prevalence in our society today of people giving just enough to get by.

These attitudes will not do. Successful people give their best; in fact, *they give more than is expected*, not less. If not, it is only a matter of time and circumstance before the "corner-cutting" will come back to haunt. As the saying goes, "Those who take short cuts only end up getting cut short."

Persevere

Just as consistency was paramount to allowing activity to accumulate into long term results, so too is perseverance. Without the ability to hang in there through "thick and thin," "the good, the bad, and the ugly," "the rain and the shine," "feast or famine," "sickness or health," "better or worse until death do us part," er, um, okay. No more. We promise this time (really). Without the ability to persevere, we rob ourselves of the accumulation of our efforts.

This is a failure mode we see with so many people. They just can't make it around the next bend in the road. So many times, success is little more than hanging on long enough for it all to come together for you. Also, the longer you persist in the pursuit of something, the more confidence and determination you will develop.

As Don Owens, Jr. said, "Many people fail in life because they believe in the adage: 'If you don't succeed, try something else.'" We have seen this many times. Someone will come into the business, give it a try, and then disappear at the first sign of resistance. They become convinced they've either found something better (the

202

next great thing), or that their old way of living wasn't *that* bad. This is sad. They are basically burning their chances to accomplish their dreams. Not that there aren't other great opportunities out there, and not that their life before the business was all bad, either. But someone who has no staying power will have no dream-achieving power. Billy Sunday said, "More men fail through lack of purpose than lack of talent." And that lack of purpose shows up in a lack of perseverance.

By the way, when people move on to the "next best thing," or bow out of challenges easily, they don't succeed in other endeavors either. This is because the opportunity wasn't the problem, the *individual* was. As Tim Marks says, "No matter where I go, there I am!" It's like the man whose grandson decides to play a trick on him by smearing limburger cheese on his moustache as he sleeps. After that, everywhere the grandfather goes that day makes him say, "This room smells!" When he decides to go outside for some fresh air he says, "It smells out here, too!" After a while he's convinced that *everything* smells! Indeed, if we are the problem, then wherever we go we'll encounter the same problem all over again. To improve, we must remember: "The best way to accelerate one's success is to double one's failure rate." When someone quits after a setback, they stop the process. This teaches them nothing. They start again, as it were, at zero. When the next obstacle comes up, they quit again, and the whole cycle starts over. All the while they are missing the best education of all; the one that comes from failing, getting up, getting better, and trying again, over and over.

There is a way to encourage perseverance, and that is to realize that all results are not visible on the outside. While it may look to outside observers that you are making no progress, there is a different story about what is happening *within* you. Many times, success requires *internal* growth long before any *external* growth shows up. This was especially true for the authors. As we began building our businesses, we were quite sure we'd be good at it. But it took a lot of listening to CD's, reading of books, and attending seminars and associating with other like-minded business owners, including very special mentors, for us to experience the internal changes that eventuated in the external changes.

Perseverance is also served by staying focused on our dreams. It is not the business we stay committed to through good times and bad, it's our *dreams*. We were shown a diagram a long time ago that depicted this:

What is shown here is that an individual's dreams aren't big enough, so they can't be seen. All that can be seen are the obstacles. The following diagram demonstrates what is necessary to fuel our perseverance and propel us to succeed: in essence, making sure our dreams are bigger than the obstacles!

We will leave this discussion on perseverance with this quote from speaker and author Dennis Waitley: "Success is almost totally dependent upon drive and persistence. The extra energy required to make another effort or try another approach is the secret of winning."

Fall in Love with Learning

We will close this chapter with an admonition that one of the most important principles for success is the desire to learn, and to learn continuously. Bill Belichick, who won three NFL Super Bowls in four years as head coach of the New England Patriots, has achieved success few in his field can match. The secret, according to author David Halberstam, is that at an early stage in his career, Belichick decided to *fall in love with learning*. That's what has to happen for success in anything, really. One has to have a burning to desire to learn more and more, so one can get better and better.

As the ancient Greek writer, Euripides wrote, "We must take care of our minds because we cannot benefit from beauty when our brains are missing." (We don't care who you are, that's funny, right there.) And as Henry Ford said, "Anyone who stops learning is old, whether at twenty or eighty. Anyone who keeps learning stays young." We would add that anyone who keeps learning keeps their business growing, too. So develop the love of learning, and never stop. Hit the Team training system with a passion. Listen to CD's over and over, read books, attend everything, and seek mentorship. As Charlie Jones said, "You are the same today that you are going to be five years from now except for two things: the people with whom you associate, and the books you read."

Personal Stories

Names: Holger and Lindsey Spiewak
Former Occupations: Quality Engineer; College Student and Nanny

The United States of America is the greatest country in the world, the land of opportunity. The rest of the world knows this. As a German citizen, having visited many different countries around the world, I can certainly attest that this is true. Being from a foreign country gives me a unique perspective on the U.S.A., and on the Team.

Originally, I came to the United States with the goal to earn a Master's Degree in Mathematics from Purdue University. With two sisters that had married U.S. Army Officers that they had met in Germany, I had had the opportunity to visit America many times before I finally decided to go to school over here. Now the plan was not to stay more than two years, as I had already received a Master's Degree to teach Math and Physics in high school in Germany. However, my destiny was not going to lead me back to my Heimatland (homeland). During my first two years at Purdue, I developed a very strong desire to stay here longer than originally planned. The opportunity came along in form of a letter sent from the Krannert Graduate School of Management at Purdue, offering me to enter into their MBA program. Perfect! After graduation, I was offered an engineering position at an automotive company in Western Michigan. There I met a guy named Bill, seemingly just another nice guy engineer, but little did I suspect how much my acquaintance with him would change my financial future.

Now, I had always been entrepreneurially minded. While at Purdue, I had a good idea and started an Internet company. To make a long story short, we crashed and burned, losing what seemed like back then, a significant amount of money. My job was a brief two year distraction from my desire to be my own boss. But the fire was burning inside and a number of lateral promotions

206

(more responsibility and same pay) don't make corporate America more attractive. Soon I started looking for other opportunities. Real estate seemed like the way to go, but the problem was trying to get a mortgage approved without being a permanent resident (at that time). The bank gave me a flat, "Sorry, but NO!" There I was, thirty-two years old, doing "pretty good" but absolutely dissatisfied with where I was in life. Then, I got an e-mail from my old buddy Bill, who at this time I had not seen in over a year. He was writing to me about an Internet business, but I wasn't very interested. I was still pinning my hopes on real estate. Bill, too, had done some real estate, so I was curious why he was now doing something with the Internet. I stood him up for the first meeting, but we finally got together. Bill proceeded for three-and-a-half hours to show me mathematical calculations on how the money worked. The problem was: he had no clue how the money worked! However, he was more excited than I had ever seen him before. I signed the paper work. I didn't know what it was, but I was in.

Now that I was in, I started to analyze this business and the one thing that really convinced me to pursue it is how the Team builds communities. At Purdue I had taken a number of statistics classes and was very familiar with the law of averages. Once I understood the Team's approach, I realized that this had to work, as long as I would not quit. Finally, I had my vehicle! A vehicle where the results were 100% correlated to what I put in. Nobody else was in control of my destiny but me.

Over the years, many things have changed, internally and externally. Internally, the greatest realization was that there is a Higher Power, an all-powerful God, who indeed is in control of my destiny. Thanks to the example of the Team leaders, I now have a personal relationship with Him. Through the Team system, and with the help of my mentors, God has made me a better person (even though he's not finished with me, yet). Externally, God blessed me with a wonderful wife, Lindsey, whom I met in the business, who is the love of my life. I could not imagine life without her. On April 1st, 2005, God blessed us with a wonderful son. It's amazing to think that if Bill had not contacted me about this business, I wouldn't have gotten free financially, wouldn't have met Lindsey, and wouldn't have my beautiful son! Talk about owing somebody a life debt! Thanks Bill!

There are many things to be grateful for but like Chris Brady always quotes, "To whom much is given, much is required." To live in these times, with an opportunity called the Team, in this country, the United States of America, the greatest country in the world, let us not take these blessings lightly, much less for granted, but go out and fulfill our destiny.

Names: George and Jill Guzzardo
Former Occupations: Physical Therapist;
Director of Nursing

I call growing up in the inner city of Chicago the "Age of Reason." I've always had a feeling there was a reason for me being in the world. I felt there was a purpose. The adventure of living in the inner city began to wear out, however. It seemed like a chaotic life-style after a while. Everyone was in a hurry, but it didn't seem like people had anywhere to go except back to where they started.

I call my years at college the "Age of Enlightenment." After meeting Jill, who was my future wife, we both pursued goals in the medical career. Jill was going into Nursing and I was going into Physical Therapy. We saw this as a way out of the city. We began to think about goals we would like to accomplish. We liked the outdoors. It symbolized freedom. So we began to dig into our careers, but gradually forgot the real reasons we had set our goals to move to the Upper Peninsula of Michigan and its beautiful outdoors. We dug in so well we began to create a rut. Our son Ryan was born and it seemed like 15 years passed like a blink of the eye.

That's when we got the call from Jill's brother Ed about a project he was working on with a guy named Orrin Woodward. We weren't sure what Ed was talking about. He said, " We're going to be millionaires." We liked what we heard and who we met. At first Orrin was very quiet. He let a guy by the name of Larry do all the talking. They tricked us into going to a leadership convention where we first saw the big picture. We knew we could be financially free with this business. We could see paying off our debts and getting more free time. We had our expectations of what it took to build this business. We all started to learn together. We watched Orrin and Laurie develop. They never *told* us to develop but they showed us by *example*. We had a lot of learning, growing and changing to do. We had to change our thinking and build a disciplined work ethic. We began to change the way we felt about people. We began to change the way we felt about ourselves. We began to think about our world views. Orrin changed because of

209

his mentoring with Pastor Robert L. Dickie. I began to change because of Orrin's change. We started to look at people differently. We broke down the wall that had formed around us. We began to love and serve people. I call *these* years being "Born Again."

Our team eventually grew. We developed many close friends. Our finances changed. We left our jobs. We became free. Our family developed an ability to communicate and appreciate one another. We began to influence others by how we had changed. We saw other families grow close, pay off their debt, and change the quality of their lives. We watched our friends develop the same results through the business training system. We observed the exponential growth of our team and saw it affect more and more people.

What happened next I call the "Age of Vision." We started to associate with Orrin and Laurie and the other leaders on the Team. We started to see a different picture about the business and how it can not only affect people but influence the communities and therefore the culture. We began to understand right and wrong values. We saw how character, trust and honesty could help educate people.

Today, we see ourselves continuing to grow with the Woodward's and the other leaders on the Team. We see the development of other leaders and our influence making a real difference not only for us, but generations to come.

I call the future the "Age of Excitement." We see challenges, but we have the tools to build on trends and take this business to new and higher levels. We see Orrin and other leaders being called to do something that has never been done before. As Orrin says, "Come join Team leadership."

We know you will see something special inside the Team.

We hope you'll come, too.

"Whatever format is used, it is important to continually reinforce the principles."
- James Hunter

"If you think the people you attract could be better, then it's time for you to improve yourself."
- John Maxwell

"Our privileges are not for our pleasure. Rather, they are for a higher purpose, to serve others."
- Chris Brady

"Leaders haven't simply practiced their vocation or profession. They've mastered it."
- Warren Bennis

"Do what you can, with what you have, where you are."
- Theodore Roosevelt

Name: CORPORATE CARTER

Quote: "This all sounds quite feasable, but I'm afraid it might create a conflict-of-interest with my job, and I'm next-in-line for the Executive III position that's opening up in HR next quarter, and I would hate to jeopardize my promotion."

Chapter 11

Business Ownership
The Specifics

The elements discussed in the previous chapter are primarily *principles* of success. They have application to the Team business, but are also required in any worthy endeavor. This chapter will be different, in that it will focus on *specifics* of building the Team business.

Edification

In the Team business, you will hear the word *edification* used a lot. Webster's Dictionary defines edifying as, "building up, establishing, or instructing and improving." When you hear the word used in connotation with the Team business, it is being applied to *people*. One of the most important specifics of building the Team business is the concept of edifying other people; in effect, building them up, or improving them with your words.

This is perhaps a foreign concept in our world of pessimism, gossip, back-stabbing, and sarcasm. People in the general society seem to take special pleasure in tearing into other people with their words. It is unfortunate, because few people seem to realize the power of the things they say, especially if they say negative things. Negative, it appears, is many times stronger than positive.

It is for this reason that we must learn to speak well of one another. By this we don't mean some false form of flattery, or anything insincere. We believe that with a little practice, and a good heart, one can learn to see the good in other people. Edifying others means finding out the good about someone and putting it into words. You would be surprised, perhaps, by how powerful a kind word to or about someone can be. We have all heard the saying: "If you can't think of something good to say, don't say anything at all." But we believe even this can be improved. "If you can't think

213

of something good to say, you'd better think harder. There is *almost always* something good to say."

You've perhaps heard also, that it's impolite to talk "behind someone's back." We disagree. We think it's extremely important to be talking behind people's backs, that is, as long as the talk is positive and complimentary. Imagine how endearing you'd become to someone if they found out that all over town, when they weren't even around, you had been singing their praises!

There is a reason for edification of other people that goes beyond the fact that it is the right thing to do and should be done anyway. In the Team business, as we've said many times, it's a business of working with people. Edification becomes the grease that helps all the gears work harmoniously together without "grinding."

For instance, imagine how much more effective someone in your up-line could be if you had properly edified them before they came to meet with some people in your organization. If you had taken the time and effort to inform your organization of your up-line's accomplishments, as well as the specific things he or she had done to help you, then chances are, your organization would be much more receptive and respectful of everything that particular up-line had to say. In this way, by building up your up-line through the process of edification, you are giving them more power to be effective in your group. It is natural for people to think, "Why should I listen to this guy?" Edification can answer that question and open their ears.

Additionally, imagine what a harmonious community of people you would build if you taught everyone to edify each other all the time. In effect, what you would be doing is "good-finding" each other. Such an environment would be energizing, positive, comfortable, and endearing. And those are the exact kinds of words people have used to describe the environment at the Team's various seminars and meetings across the country. "There's just something different about you guys," they say. "It's just something you can feel in the air." A big part of that "feeling" is that the Team business owners have learned to edify and encourage each other.

Edification cannot be mechanical. It can't be something that you do because you know that you are supposed to. Rather, it must be true and sincere. It must come from the heart. We must all become good at finding the good in others. If we have trouble doing this, perhaps we have issues with our pride that we need to address.

One of our favorite quotes is by Harry Truman, "You would be surprised how much you could accomplish if you didn't care who got the credit." Edification is about giving credit away. Build others up, so that they can be more effective, and perhaps even help you in return.

Someone once asked if edification might be lying. After all, saying good things about people is choosing to ignore the "less than good things" that could be said about any of us. Is this an error of omission? The answer is no. There is nothing wrong with choosing to see the good in people. Edification is the art of identifying what an individual's strengths are and then "packaging" that person properly. A person's strengths should be put in the proper light; he or she should not be given false strengths. In building the business, one needs to have the proper "package" for each of his or her up-line business partners. In this way, he or she can be properly edified based upon the strengths brought to the building of the team.

Duplication

We already touched on duplication a few times earlier in this book. We couldn't help it. That's because duplication is such a big part of what make the Team business so special.

When a business is built properly, business owners are plugged into the training system. The training system becomes their source of information. They learn to listen to CD's to answer their questions. They learn to read books to improve themselves. And they attend seminars and major functions to get inspired, get recognized, and learn the information that will be vital to helping them move on. The key here is that the *system* becomes their source, not the *up-line business owner*. If a business owner builds his or her team properly by plugging them entirely into the training system, then that business owner has developed what Robert Kiyosaki calls a "B-Type" business. This is a business in which a *system* runs the business instead of the *owner*. Why is this important? Precisely because the concept of wealth is not just money, it must also be accompanied with enough free time to enjoy that money. When business owners build businesses properly founded in the system, they have set themselves up not only for income, but for time to enjoy it.

Duplication also sets up a pattern where the business grows without the direct inputs of the business owner, after a while. In the beginning, the business owner must show every plan, sell every product, and move every ticket. But eventually, other people copy that business owner's example, and begin doing the work also. This is duplication. And as we stated earlier: the better the example, the better the duplication. Properly built, using the strategies of depth and the training system, business owners will eventually see their businesses spread to people they have never met and to geographic locations to which they have never been. This can develop into geometric, outward growth. This is the power of compounding at its best. It is at this point that the business owner has a true B-Type business and begins getting some of his or her time back.

Because of the huge multiplication available through the structure of the Team business, it is important for the business owner to think about the concept of duplication in everything he or she does. At every turn, the business owner should ask him or herself, "Is this duplicatable? Would I want a thousand people doing what I'm about to do?"

There have been many business owners who have decided to do things "their way." They get a crazy notion here or put a twist on things there and wonder why their business isn't growing. Or they wonder why their whole team is so off track. Being just a little off-track at the beginning of the journey can result in arriving miles away from the target later on.

There is another way to explain this. In *The Cashflow Quadrant*, Robert Kiyosaki compares the poor and middle-class to the wealthy. One of the chief differences between them is how they generate their income. The poor and middle-class are taught that it is all about *them*. *They* must be effective, smart, educated, capable, and indispensable. Whereas the wealthy realize it should not be about them at all, eventually. Wealth comes from a *system* that runs a business or *investments*. The person becomes less and less a factor in the equation as success mounts, and wealth streams in systematically. This cannot happen if the business is built upon the individual's constant inputs, tweaks, and adjustments, or if the person is indispensable to the income on an ongoing basis. In effect, the wealthy take themselves out of the picture and let systematic income generation become the whole picture. The poor and middle-class try to make *themselves* the whole picture. Understanding this concept, we can then see the extreme importance of making sure that everything we do is duplicatable and systematic. The more of "us" that we pump into it, the more of "us" that will be required to generate the income and the less systematic it will be. Again, look at the master copy. Always make sure it is worth duplicating, and therefore setting up systematic success.

Promotion

Promotion is the ability to encourage others to take steps in the business that will be beneficial to them, specifically the steps of getting involved in the training system. Let's face it: people are programmed to try to get by on minimums. "What's the least I can do and get the most out of it?" "How little can I pay for it?" etc. But success doesn't work that way. No pain, no gain. No investment, no return.

In the Team business, one of the great advantages is that the expenses and investments required are laughably low. On any kind of scale compared to any kind of conventional business, the amount of money that is required to build a Team business doesn't even show up! But because this business is unconventional, people many times don't evaluate their investments here as investments. They begin to think of them as expenses. A painter who pays thousands of dollars for equipment will hesitate when it comes to buying a CD. A lawyer who has tens of thousands of dollars invested into his education and accreditations will baulk at buying a ticket to a seminar! The ability to overcome these natural tendencies of the uninformed, and help them become informed, is what we call promotion.

Promotion is accomplished by helping the other person see the Team training system's stack of benefits. You have to help them see the value in investing. In the words we've used before, you have to help them understand "what's in it for them." This involves showing them the relevance of why they should attend that next event or get involved with the CD's of the Week program.

One way to do this is to tie whatever is being promoted to their dream. Help them see how taking the appropriate steps in the business relates to accomplishing the dream(s) that got them interested in the business in the first place.

Another approach involves matching the promotion to the person. If you know that the person to whom you are promoting something is a detailed individual, be sure and explain to them the details they will be receiving from attending that seminar. If they are a fun-seeking people person, be sure and promote the large crowd that will be there and all the fun that will be had. If they are casual, easy-going, and soft-spoken, let them know you really want them to go and are looking forward to spending the time with them. The final type of person, the aggressive type, should be told that all the leaders will be there! When promoting to specific personality types, be sincere. Don't play games. Just help them see which part of the event or tool is the most relevant for their particular temperament.

It all comes down to creating a hunger on their part. You must try to show them what is in it for them, and why it will have relevance. It is important that they feel that you are trying to help them, not trying to sell them on something. Be sure and establish rapport, and show them that you care. If they come up with objections, take the time to work through them, in much the same way as we discussed in the section on Follow-Through. Belief and conviction and excitement on your part will carry the day. Promotion requires posture, just like everything else in this business. It isn't important that *they* believe it, it's only important that they believe that *you* believe in it. Once they experience things for themselves, they will believe it too! If not, at least you did your part and "got them to the campfire." If they don't like the roasted marshmallows, at least you got them there to discover that for themselves.

We don't want our business partners incurring any unnecessary expenses. Remember, they are in this business to make some money. We must always be trying to help them accomplish that. What we are interested in helping them do is invest wisely for the best possible return on investment. If they are not going to use what you are trying to promote, then by all means, do not promote it! Remember the axiom we've been referring back to throughout this book: what's in it for them!? Always keep that in mind, and your promotion will be spot on.

Promotion is absolutely essential to building a big business. As one successful business owner once said, "You must get good at promoting in order to have a big business. And if you're *not* good at promoting, you'll have a big business once you *get* good at promoting!"

Mentors

There are two sure ways to failure: listening to everyone, and listening to no one. The route to success is somewhere in between. Personal experience is certainly an effective teacher, but trial and error can be painful, and is always slower than learning from someone else. However, no one person is infallible, and nobody has all the answers. Therefore, following a single individual can be narrow at best, dangerous at worst. What is best is to find a multitude of counselors (as the Bible recommends) that are likeminded and unified in their message. They will still have differing personalities, perspectives, and experiences, but their information and experiences can be invaluable to others traversing the same path. The Team training system provides access to exactly that type of "unified diversity." Every speaker on a Team stage, or on a recording, has achieved success to a level high enough to warrant their invitation to present their experiences and knowledge to others. The range of teachers in the Team training system is as diverse as the population of the United States itself. But the message and information these achievers share is spot on. It works. And it can work for others who learn what these people have learned and do what they have done.

Finding and listening to mentors is one of the most misunderstood, unknown, and overlooked parts of success. Most of us can think back to someone in our lives who had a special impact on us: hopefully a parent, but also maybe a teacher, relative, or coach. That person might have seen more in us than we had previously seen in ourselves. Maybe he or she expected the best out of us and wouldn't listen to our excuses. Those types of people in our lives, in a way, were early mentors.

Professional success of the highest kind, and especially in the Team business, will require mentorship. Mentorship is the process of utilizing the experience of someone who has gone before you. As the saying goes, "The best route to success is in the footsteps of someone who has gone before you."

In all business, there is a mine field of things that can happen between initial excitement and success. A mentor becomes your tour guide through that mine field. What is the best way to learn? Through experience – *other people's* experience. That's the role of a mentor, to provide that experience.

So the first thing to know when building the Team business is that you are going to want to seek out mentorship. At first, this will probably be limited to the training materials in the system. It might also include the person or persons who were involved in getting you started in the business. But as you perform, you will get noticed by those in the up-line, and begin to qualify for special meetings and even one-on-one time with your up-line leadership. Take advantage of these situations! One great piece of advice or perspective from someone who has prospered in this business might be just the nugget you need to move on!

Over time, it will become obvious to you who your main mentor in the business will be. There isn't any hard, fast rule about this. There is nothing formalized. But this is good, because as a result, you may have the privilege of several mentors as you rise up through the levels of success in the Team business. This is one thing that sets our business apart. In much of corporate America, mentorship is not even talked about, much less practiced. But in the Team business it is a way of life.

As you get time around those that have gone further than you in the business, take advantage of it. Have your questions ready. And be ready to listen. Many times people think that time with their mentor is a chance to blab about all that they've been doing. Chances are your mentor already *knows* how you've been doing. He or she is fully aware of the measurements of your business that we talked about in Chapter 9. The purpose of meeting with your mentor is primarily to *gain perspective*. Remember that how you see things is critical. Your up-line mentor can help you see things in the correct light. They will be able to help you make sense of things you haven't seen or understood before. They can help re-frame your challenges so that you see them in the most advantageous way.

Another thing to keep in mind when communicating with your mentor is to do your own thinking. What we mean by this is that you should think about your challenges and obstacles and come up with your own conclusions, then bounce those off your mentor to check the quality of your thinking on the subject. "Am I seeing this correctly? Am I thinking about this right? Here's what's happening, and here's what I think I've got to do about it, what do *you* think?" This is the correct way to take the most advantage of your mentor's experience.

Be careful when dealing with your mentor to be open and honest. We all want to look good. We all want to impress those for whom we have the most respect. But don't just show up and "put on a good face." Don't say, "I know," to everything your mentor recommends. It's okay *not* to know. That's why you've pursued a mentor in the first place, so that you could learn to know what you didn't even know you didn't know.

Conversely, don't show up and "dump" on your mentor. They are not there to hear a bunch of complaints and whining. They want to deal with people who are committed to success, honest about their current abilities, and hungry to improve. This will require clear, honest communication.

The subject of mentorship is enormous, and interestingly, it is very lightly treated in popular success literature. That is one reason we wrote the book *Launching a Leadership Revolution*. In its pages, we deal with the subject of mentorship in excruciating detail. It may be helpful for you to read those sections to gain a deeper understanding of what you should be seeking from your mentors. But suffice it to say that seeking, finding, and utilizing a mentor is fundamental to achieving the highest levels of success in the Team business.

Counsel Up-Line

This topic goes along with what we said above about seeking and utilizing a mentor. The term "counsel up-line" is most often used to indicate the value of free advice. In the business world outside of the Team business, trade secrets and strategies are closely guarded. Cards are held close to the chest. Everything is competitive and there is very little sharing of information which could jeopardize a successful enterprise by enabling competitors. But with the Team business, those that have gone before you and have gained experience and success actually benefit from sharing their secrets with you. For this reason, each of us has individuals in our up-line that are more successful than we are in the business and who are available for our access. These are the mentors of whom we spoke before.

We often recommend that business owners should counsel up-line before taking action in the business for which they are unsure. It is also recommended that all major purchases be run past the up-line before making them. This is where people sometimes get confused. "Do I have to ask permission to be able to buy something?" Certainly not. Each business owner runs his own business and is free to do whatever he or she wants to do, within the rules. Counseling up-line is not asking for permission, it is asking for free advice. Think back to the times in your life where you chose poorly in some circumstance. What would the value have been of having someone in your life who had a vested interest in your well-being, who could have been consulted beforehand about the situation? The answer? Priceless. That's what an up-line can provide: priceless perspective and advice that the business owner can then choose to follow, or not.

It's a good idea to counsel up-line any time you feel like "tweaking the system" or modifying the pattern, even in the slightest ways. That's because, chances are, your innovation has already been tried, and your more experienced up-line can shed light on what occurred and why it may or may not be a good idea. Additionally, if your idea is a good one, your up-line can take it to his or her up-line and ultimately it can get taught across the entire team, which only helps everyone!

Cross-Lining

Imagine that you invested years of effort into raising your son. You taught him how to throw a ball, you were there when he took his first steps, and you had "the talk" with him about the birds and the bees. Then imagine that some other person started taking your son aside and teaching him things that were *your responsibility* to teach him. Imagine that this person, who had no authority to do so, even taught things that were in conflict with the values you had worked so hard to instill in your child (and no, we are not trying to bash colleges here, but . . .). How would that make you feel?

We use that example as a way to introduce the subject of cross-lining in the Team business, because cross-lining is one of those topics that is almost impossible to understand until it happens to you. What is meant by cross-lining in the business is very near the example we just gave. Except replace "your son" in the example with "a business owner in your organization."

We are not sure why it happens. Maybe it's some odd corner of human nature. But people like to stick their noses where they don't belong. That's the beginning of cross-lining. Somebody in a different organization, a "cross-line" organization (hence the term), begins building a relationship or sharing information with someone who is neither in their up-line nor down-line.

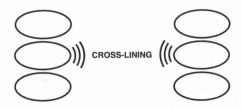

When this happens, nothing good can come from it. There is always a damaging result.

Let us give an example. Let's say two cross-line business owners strike up a conversation out in the hall at an Open Meeting. One business owner says to the other, "How's it going?" to which the other replies, "Great! It's growing faster than ever!" This might seem like a pretty harmless interchange. But what if the first business owner isn't experiences rapid business growth at the moment? He or she walks away thinking, "What's wrong with *me*? Why isn't *my* business growing as fast as *his* business? Actually, what's wrong with my up-line? Maybe if I were on *his* team instead of the one I'm on, *I'd* be growing faster, too." We've seen this happen time and time again. The other thing that this interchange could cause is doubt on the part of the faster growing business owner. He or she might walk away from that exchange thinking, "Wow. That person doesn't seem to be doing too well. Maybe I'm just getting lucky right now with my business growth. Maybe it won't last." We agree. The conclusions these two fictional characters are making are overblown, short-term, uninformed, and incorrect. But people don't always have the discernment to see that for themselves, especially when they are the ones in the situation.

A worse type of cross-lining is the intentional kind. This is where, normally, a business owner has been in the business a while and begins feeling comfortable. He or she thinks the rules of cross-lining somehow don't apply to *them*. So they start "chatting up" with every cross-line business owner they can. They might even be bold enough to start asking business advice or for private business information. "Say, how did your CD's of the Week count do this week?" or "So how many people have you guys got here at this seminar?" or "How are you guys contacting people?" This is a very poisonous situation and should be stopped immediately. Why? Because it is impolite, it's unfair to the up-line who have worked with that person and invested their time into them, and it's just not any of their business!

Now don't get us wrong. The idea of cross-lining doesn't mean you can't talk to people that are not on your team. It doesn't mean you can't be part of the camaraderie that the being around cross-line organizations provides. It doesn't mean you have to be up-tight and act all weird around people who are not part of your up-line or down-line organization. But what it does mean is that you should keep your interactions appropriate. Show respect to the people that are mentoring those business owners. Be a team player. And actually, be more focused on your *own* team than on somebody else's. Taking it back to the example we started this section with: raise your own kids!

There is another aspect of cross-lining that we should point out. Those that grow the fastest, biggest businesses simply don't have time for it. They are too involved serving their own team, working with their own business partners, that they don't have time to mess with anybody else's. It has been our experience that we don't have all the time we would like to spend with each of the partners on our own teams as it is, much less get involved with those *not* on our teams.

Communication in our type of business should always be within the line of sponsorship. That means either up-line, or down-line. Communication with cross-line business owners should be friendly, encouraging, and appropriate. Enough said.

Negative Up-Line

There is another little specific to building the Team business that we should now explain, and thankfully, it is easier to explain than cross-lining! This is the concept that when you have something "negative" to say, that you say it *up-line* and not *down-line*. You might be amazed at how often people find something negative to say, and then run out and tell their group about it. This does nothing but cause doubt and consternation in their own team. It's like spewing poison onto a plant you're trying to grow!

Instead, if you have an issue, or something that is less than positive and uplifting, take it up-line. Chances are they can handle it. More importantly, they will know how to help you handle it. And remember, it's not "negative" (i.e. "whining" and "complaining") if you come truly seeking a *solution*.

Goal Setting

To make sure that you are productive in the business and not simply busy, it will be important to make goal setting a part of your business habits. Here is a brief excerpt from *Launching a Leadership Revolution* on this concept of goal setting:

> In the words of the hockey great Wayne Gretzky, "You will miss 100% of the shots you don't take." We must assume he was referring to shots on a *goal*. Without specific goals at which to direct our energies and ambitions, our efforts will at best be wandering generalities.
>
> The story is told of two men who set out to accomplish similar results. One invested the effort to properly set goals and the other did not. At the end of a period of time, both men had worked diligently, but the one who had set a specific goal by far outperformed the other man. This is because everything the goal setting man did was unconsciously directed toward his goal. If there was something to be done, it was first determined if it would assist him in accomplishing his goal. If it would, then he did it. If it would not help him hit his goal, he would not do it. You see; the goal setting man had the advantage of priorities over the non-goal setting man. He also had the advantage of channeling his efforts more effectively through the power of focus. On any given day there are a number of "good" things to be done. There are only a few "great" things to be done. And there can only be one "best" thing

to do. A leader must know and do the "best" things on a regular basis.

Goal setting is a discipline. It should never be a haphazard affair. There are several components to the proper setting of goals that every leader should embody. Goals must be:

1. Specific
2. Written
3. Set in Stone
4. Measurable
5. Realistic
6. Provide Motivation
7. In Line With Priorities and Values
8. Prominent
9. For a Specific Time Period

In the Team business we talk about running for goals in "thirty day sprints." Proper goal setting coincides with the measurements we talked about in Chapter 9. How many plans are you going to show this month? What will your ticket count be? How many per each leg? And what will your CD's of the Week count be? Finally, what will your product volume be? Remember to keep things in the order of Conquer (plans shown and depth built), Fortify (people "on system"), and Domesticate (product volume and DOT1/STEP). And don't set too many goals or get too complicated about it. It is useless to focus on many things at once. For most of us, we find that we do better when we focus upon one main goal at a time. All the other goals that align with it will fall into place eventually if we hit the main goal.

So set goals each month, counsel with your up-line mentor(s) about them, and run for them with all you've got. If you should miss a goal, re-set it and try again. You will get better and better at goal setting as you gain experience. You will learn the futility of setting goals too high, and the impotence of setting goals too low. Goals set too high will discourage you. Conversely, goals set too low will not motivate you.

Money Management

There is a slightly humorous saying that rings true: "The only way to get wealthy is to make more than you spend, and also to spend less than you earn." This is only too simple. But almost nobody follows it.

In our years with the Team business, we have seen countless people enter the business because they need to make more money. So far so good. But after a while, the reason they need to make more money becomes obvious: *they waste the money they make.*

A common fallacy in people's minds goes something like this, "Well, I'll be out of all this money trouble as soon as I start making more money. That's why I joined the Team." And to a degree, that is a correct statement. However, it is not a correct statement if the person has no *discipline* in handling his or her finances. Read the following statement very carefully: **If you do not develop financial discipline and self-control, you will never be wealthy, no matter how much money you make.** Making more money is never the solution to someone in this condition. Why, you might ask? Because *a lack of money* is not the *problem*, therefore *an increase in money* cannot be the *solution*. *A lack of discipline* is the problem. Therefore, only an *increase in discipline* can be the solution.

For this reason, the Team trainings system focuses a lot on developing self-discipline and maturity. The system also talks about money and its proper management. In fact, it might be fair to say that the Team business will require you to get and continue an education in four categories:

1. The business particulars
2. Success principles
3. People
4. Money

To begin with, being irresponsible with money is downright dishonest. If you write a check to someone, the moment you sign your name you are in effect giving your word that the money is *there,* immediately available. Bouncing a check is the same as lying. Now, we understand that banks and people make mistakes, and we've probably all had the occasion upon which an error causes a bounced check. But that's not what we're talking about here. We're talking about dishonesty, and far too many people have somehow gotten it into their heads that bouncing checks is "acceptable." It is not. There is no excuse.

People waste their money in all sorts of different ways, as we'll demonstrate in the next section. To succeed financially, both husband and wife must learn to live on less than they earn, period. This may involve cutting back on the number of restaurant visits, cancelling the cable television, or the extra channels, or begining to live on a budget. This is a critical area in which to counsel with your up-line and determine how you are doing to this point. Your up-line can lay out a game plan to help you maximize what you are getting out of your current income and make sure you plug the holes.

Here is why this is necessary, and it is a mindset that the average person out there doesn't seem to understand: money is your slave. It will do exactly what you tell it to do. If you want it to fill you with junk food for the body, or junk food for the mind, it will do so perfectly. However, if you can be taught to use your money for *productive* things, your money will actually go out and bring you back *more* money! Too often, people waste their money when they should be leveraging it by putting it to work for them. With the Team training system, people have found a way they can plant seeds of a future financial harvest. Most of these seeds involve the planting of time. But some amount of investment money along the way will be necessary, even though it is quite small when compared to conventional businesses and their capital requirements. Learn to treat money with respect and don't waste it.

On the detail side of things, upon starting your Team business, you should immediately open up a new and separate checking account from anything you had previous to the business. After all, you are running a business now, and it should be treated as such. It should have its own separate finances. Put your income from the business into that account, and draw your expenses for the business from that account. This will make things easier at tax time, also. To start your business, it will need to be funded. Put a chunk of money in that account to get started. If possible, make sure it is enough that you can invest properly in tools and events and any other little expenses that might accrue along the way, as you begin building your business.

Also, keep good records. Keep track of miles driven, and keep all receipts for anything incurred while in the honest pursuit of a profit. Tools, travel, products to demonstrate, etc. are all usually deductible expenses. We are not accountants, but we have several very good ones we use as our advisors and tax specialists and preparers. You should too. In the beginning, your business will simply be a sole proprietorship, and will involve a Schedule C attachment to your normal tax return. As you grow to higher incomes in the business, (approximately the time you leave your job and make the business your living) you will want to incorporate. Let your tax specialists advise you on how best to do that when the time comes. Your up-line can also offer some insight.

Another category of money management is how to spend your money as it starts to come rolling in as a result of your efforts in the Team business. The best idea is to set a business goal. Then when you hit that goal, assuming you have also hit a corresponding financial goal (again, counsel up-line), you can purchase that item or trip as a reward. That way, each reward you earn through the business becomes a yardstick that measures how many people you have helped along the way. Just avoid the damaging temptation to make the reward greater than the financial reward directly related to the goal. Buying things you can't yet afford, just because you hit a minimum business goal would be directionally incorrect. This is where your financial discipline comes to the rescue.

Your money should ultimately get split in several directions: the money you give away, the money you save, the money you invest, and the money off of which you live. There are many great books in our system that delve into this area of learning how to manage and leverage your finances, and can help you determine the proper proportion for you for each of these categories. Just remember, money should work for *you*, you should not work for *it*. Waste it and you'll be its slave. Deploy it widely, and it'll be yours.

Investment vs. Expense

There is a big difference between *spending* money and *investing* money. Once money is spent, it is gone forever. Money invested, however, should bring a return. To go the farthest in life financially, one should put as much money as possible into investing and as little as possible into spending. Unfortunately, people generally live in the exact opposite way.

Allow us to illustrate with a fun example. You will get more out of this if you play along, and you'll probably enjoy it. (We certainly did.) In the spaces that follow, mark down the average monthly amount you spent (before you got involved in this business) on each of the items listed. For things that you purchased perhaps only once or twice a year, divide the one-time purchase cost by twelve months, and write the average monthly cost of that item. Total your numbers at the bottom.

Before getting exposed to the Team business, how much money do you estimate that you spent *per month* on each of the following items?

1. cable or satellite television   _____
2. movie rentals   _____
3. newspaper subscriptions   _____
4. magazine subscriptions   _____
5. music CD's   _____
6. movie purchases or DVD's   _____
7. website subscriptions   _____
8. cups of coffee   _____
9. soda, pop, or soft drinks   _____
10. snacks at a gas station, etc.   _____
11. seeing a movie at a theatre   _____
12. attending a sporting event   _____
13. attending a concert   _____

(continued on next page)

14. car audio equipment   _____
15. home audio equipment   _____
16. home video equipment   _____
17. restaurant meals, including tips _____
18. cigarettes   _____
19. alcohol   _____
20. sports league participation _____
21. any other general recreation _____
22. other hobbies, golf, etc.   _____

Grand Total, Average Monthly Expenditure_____

We could conceivably continue this list indefinitely, but we'll stop with that. How did you do? Is your total surprising? It is for most people. We were shocked at the amount of money we were blowing on a monthly basis without really realizing it, and worse, without really *accomplishing anything*!

Most of the items in that list are not bad in and of themselves. In fact, most of us enjoy nearly all of them. But it is the accumulated total amount of money we are wasting that should shock us awake. Most people squander a great portion of their income on things they only *sort of want*, and therefore never accomplish their dreams, the things they *really want* in life.

The principle of investing is best served by the farmer's creed: never eat your seed wheat. Too many people blow what power money could provide by spending it on things that don't get them anywhere.

As you become more and more involved in the Team business, it will be important for you to resist the urge to "nickel and dime" your business. Remember, this is a business built on duplication, and the only way to achieve wealth and freedom is to develop a business where the *system* runs it instead of you. This will require that you plant some "seed wheat," in this case, tools (CD's, books, pamphlets, etc.) that can be planted in the lives of people, including yourself.

First of all, don't get confused when you subscribe to the CD's of the Week program or buy tickets to a seminar by thinking that you are *spending* money. You are *investing*, not spending. It strikes us as strange, but we've seen people who have taken the above test and realized they were wasting a couple thousand dollars a month on items that weren't getting them ahead, but those same people baulk at the price of gaining a true education through the Team! The first place to invest your money is *yourself!* Any CD you need, any book, or any conference you need to attend is an investment in *you*. There can be no better investment. You are worth at least as much as all those needless items in the list above. What is more important: soft drinks and cable television, or improving your mind?

Secondly, don't be cheap when it comes to planting seeds. If you want a good harvest, you must have a good stock of seeds to plant. Tools on hand are seeds you plant in the lives of other people to grow your business. You will hear talk of something called a "tool trunk." This is the stock of tools any serious business owner should have in his or her car (hence trunk) for the purpose of distributing to others. A true business owner should have the right amount of tools to allow him or her to do the job correctly. Picture a carpenter who frames homes for a living. Imagine him showing up to the job site with less than an adequate supply of tools. "Can I borrow your nail gun? Are you using that level? Hey buddy, can I strap on your tool belt for a while?" It doesn't happen. Equally silly is a Team business owner who has an incomplete stock of tools in his or her car. Professionals show up prepared.

A proper stock of tools ought to include at least the following:

1. First-night materials
2. Second night materials
3. Making the Names List Brochures
4. Registration forms and the SA 4400
5. Copies of the top 5 books
6. Top 50 packs
7. Brochures
8. Extra CD's, teaching and story types
9. Board and easel

10. DVD's

11. Tickets to the next function

How much of each is enough? That will be based upon your activity level and desire. The faster you want to go, the better your trunk should be stocked. It's much cheaper to invest in a few tools than it is to meet a quality prospective business owner and be short the one thing that might have made the difference in involving them in the business! So be a professional and stock up.

Then, once you've stocked your trunk and would be proud to show it to your up-line, get to work making it work for you. Everywhere you go, create opportunities to hand out materials to your team. Obviously, showing a bunch of plans will begin this process, as that will require first-night packs, and then additional materials as you guide people into the business. But never underestimate the need your partners in the business have for the correct information and inspiration, and be sure to promote tools to them every chance you get.

Understand the difference between investment and expense, and maximize your investments while minimizing your expenses. Then make the system work for you.

Husband and Wife Teams

Building your business will present many wonderful opportunities to you, in essence, "opportunities within the opportunity." One of these will be the chance to work in close harmony with your spouse.

Okay, so that may or may not excite you yet. But rest assured; many have found that the business becomes a wonderful point of commonality between the marriage partners. Where perhaps lives were diverging before, the Team business can be something that brings a family closer together.

This may take time, however. It's natural for two people to "warm up" to ideas at different rates. For many couples, one of the individuals in the couple was ready for marriage before the other. Quite possibly it was the same with having children. The business

234

is no different. Normally one of the spouses "sees it" and the other spouse eventually agrees to come along too. In this situation, it is important that the excited spouse doesn't "push" or pressure the non-interested spouse. Just remain positive, get the business working, and applaud any steps the uninvolved spouse takes to help in the business. Given this kind of space, both spouses almost always get up to speed and get excited about the Team business opportunity.

Next you get to learn to work together as a team! One of the most important teams you will have to build in your business is the *husband and wife team*. This will require you to use all the people skills you're learning in the business on *each other* (a novel idea). Many times people ask us, "What is my role in the business?" The answer to this is that there aren't any solid rules on what the husband does and what the wife does. The only answer is, "Whatever it takes so that the two of you get your business growing." That may sound oversimplified, but the fact is that it is much more important to ask about *attitudes* than it is to ask about *roles*. If you each have the attitude that you will do your part to make the business grow, whatever that is at any given point in time, then your business will do just fine. You'll eventually fall into roles that work the best for both of you within your husband-wife team. Along the way, you will find that you have "gotten it together, together."

Building As a Single

So what if your spouse never gets involved in the business, or what if you don't have a spouse? In either of these cases you will have the chance to build the business as a single. There are some benefits to this, of course (for one, you get to make all decisions about how to spend the money), as well as some differences.

Building the business as a single will require you to cover all aspects of the business yourself, obviously. This means you will need to be sure and be organized and deal properly with the *details* of the business (tracking system counts, product volume, setting up customers, etc.), but also be charging ahead in the growth parts of the business (rotating the Five Step Pattern, etc.). You will essentially be wearing multiple hats. This is okay, because we've seen time and time again individuals who have built big businesses as singles, whether male or female, married or unmarried.

There are a few things to be aware of as you build the business as a single. One is to be very businesslike and make sure the impression isn't accidentally made which would suggest your "contact" is anything other than business. The other is to talk about your up-line a lot, which will help to increase the feel of professionalism and help the prospects understand this is a business proposal. Also, be sure never to get yourself into a position where you could even be *accused* of false intentions. If you, as a single, are working with a business partner who is married, go out of your way to develop a friendship with the couple together, especially if the excited one of the couple is your opposite gender.

The biggest thing is not to get hung-up on the fact that you're building the business as a single. Be sure and read all of the books that come down through the system, even those dealing with husband-wife relationships. This is because you will have people in your organization that will be married, and you'll want to understand and be able to help them. Likewise, if you're married and reading this thinking it doesn't apply to you, you will need to learn to deal with singles that will come into your business. The bottom line is that the Team business is a people business, not a couples business. Focus upon helping other people prosper and you'll do just fine yourself, married or not.

Building Out of Town

Building a business at a location many hours from your house is called an "out of town" group. Normally, a group is considered out of town if it is too far away to drive to and back in a single evening.

There are many purposes of building out of town groups. First of all, you or someone in your organization simply knows some good people in another town or state. Also, having a group that is not geometrically limited "smoothes out" the effects of localized economic issues. For instance, if the southwest United States has recently been ravaged by hurricanes, the houses in those towns have been blown down, and you will suddenly find that rotating the Five Step Pattern doesn't work so well there. Financially speaking, having a group spread out across the country minimizes the impact of localized calamities on the strength of your business. Next, having groups at a distance will be one of the best ways to learn how to find and develop leaders. If you can't be there to do all the work yourself, you'll have to learn how to leverage the training system and develop some leaders in that area. This, in turn, will make you better at building your local businesses. Another interesting thing that occurs at a distance is that your credibility is enormous. Prospects think that anybody who would cover a great distance to build a business *must* be committed, and they usually tend to be more receptive to what the out of town "expert" has to say. Finally, having groups spread out across the country provides a great opportunity for a little geometric competition. As we like to say, "Competition breeds cooperation." Groups at distances from each other will watch each other and naturally try to be "your biggest group." This is healthy and should be fostered, carefully and within reason, of course.

Building distance groups will require a commitment on your part. You are looking primarily for a business owner in that location that will do the work when you are not there. If they don't or won't, you haven't got the right people with which to build a distance group. For a distance organization to grow, it will require ongoing feeding. This means that you should travel to them on a regular basis. There may or may not be a Team Open Meeting or Seminar in that location. If there are, by all means, utilize these events and leverage them to assist you in building your business there. But they will never grow your business for you. You must still take the time to travel to those groups and make them grow. Use the Team events to supplement your actions. If there are no Team events in that area, simply build your group big enough that the Team will begin scheduling them there. As the movie Field of Dreams famously said, "Build it, and they will come." In any case, distance groups require a heavy dose of the training system.

Always arrive with copious quantities of CD's and books, and any other tools they will need to get their business going. The power of the training system is perhaps *even more* required for building distance groups than for local groups: if you don't water the group thoroughly with tools, it will not grow.

Personal Story

Names: Ed and Lynette Zentner
Former Occupations: Engineering Manager,
Self-Employed Business Owner; Divisional Business
Planner in Automotive Industry

Having been raised by parents who immigrated to this country in search of a better life, I was familiar with work ethic. For thirty-eight years I understood the Industrial Age concept of "go to school, get good grades and get a safe, secure job at a big company with good benefits." I had done that, but I always felt like there was something missing. After obtaining an engineering degree and gaining employment in the automotive industry with one of the Big Three automotive manufacturers, (while I was operating my own lawn irrigation business I had started when I was sixteen), I was not too concerned about income. However, my wife Lynette and I felt we needed an edge on our corporate colleagues, so we both obtained our Masters Degrees in Business. Since we were not fiscally irresponsible, we had no major debt outside of our home, but we also didn't have any time together or with our expanding family. Having moved through various positions and promotions, both within and eventually outside the original company I started with, I "enjoyed" (facetiously) the stress of managing both engineers and an automotive supply manufacturing facility that was losing money each month. The hours required to take care of business (60-70 hrs/wk) meant even less time with Lynette and our two daughters, not to mention running my irrigation business. There had to be more to life than driving to day care and rushing off to work each day. The rut was becoming unbearable. The search was on. I was looking. I considered real estate, storage facilities, and several other options to generate passive income, prior to being introduced to the Team concept.

Upon being invited to a presentation of the Team business concept by one of the engineers who worked for me (Tim Marks), I could see the light bulb turn on in my head and I knew I could never go back to the way I had previously thought. I didn't expect that success would be without effort. I was willing to learn what it took, but now I had people and a system that were in place to support the climb up a totally different ladder of success, one that was based on a Win-Win concept.

Since becoming Independent Business Owners utilizing the Team Approach strategy, Lynette was able to come home from her corporate career, in Marketing, within the first year. I closed my irrigation business after my prior commitments had been met and we both began to enjoy a bit more sanity in our lives. Having been able to help others become "job optional" through this business has been truly rewarding and has positively impacted not only our family's lives, but the lives of many others along the way. After about four years of building this business, I was able to say good-bye to my corporate career altogether, and focus on living life and helping others have the same opportunity.

In a time when corporations are downsizing, benefits are being cut, and job security is nowhere to be seen, it's nice to know that there are still opportunities out there, with people of integrity to work with. If you're willing to step out of the box and be willing to learn about what you don't know, the potential is unlimited!

"You hit home runs not by chance, but by preparation."
- Roger Maris

"If you want to arrive at your destination, you have to keep the engines running."
- Burke Hedges

"Success is largely a matter of holding on after others have let go."
- John L. Mason

"You can't have success without discipline."
- Steve Price

"If you have a dream and don't follow it, you'll regret it for a long, long time."
- Norm Brodsky

Name: BILLY FAKER

Quote: "I'm doing pretty good. Why would I wanna do somethin' like this when I'm making good money down at the Toothpick Factory?"

Chapter 12

Conclusion
Seize the Day

Psychiatrist Alfred Adler said, "The chief danger in life is that you may take too many precautions." Another famous quote says, "To dare not is to risk the most."

Author Alexander Lockhart tells the following story:

"One day, the Apaches [in the time of the Old West] attacked a cavalry unit and captured the army paymaster's safe. They had never seen a safe before, but they knew it held a large amount of gold. But, there was one problem. They had no idea how to open the safe. They pounded on it with stones, whacked at it with their tomahawks, roasted it in a hot fire, soaked it in the river, and even tried blasting it open with gunpowder, but nothing seemed to work. Finally, the Apache chief had an idea. 'Throw it off the cliff,' he shouted to his men. This would surely break open the safe when it hit the rocks hundreds of feet below. Much to their disappointment, however, it did not work. All that happened was that one of the wheels broke off the safe.

Totally frustrated, they gave up and left the treasure safe in the ravine. Later, members of the army found the safe, and within a few minutes with the correct combination, opened the safe and found the gold still inside.

Most of us are like that safe. To find the treasures that lie deep inside of you, the right combination must first be found. Once unlocked, you will find the great untapped reserves of potential."

We believe that the Team business is a lot like the correct combination for that safe. Perhaps you've tried many things in your life to unlock your potential, but try as you may, like the Apaches and that safe of old, you could not unlock your greatness. You could never seem to find the way to take yourself all the way up to your full potential. The Team business has the ability to unlock all that is in you. But you've got to turn the dial. You've got to use the Team business to unlock the safe of golden potential deep inside of you. Remember, the Team business is not just a plan; it's a *solution*.

A Bike and a Jet

As we come to the end of this book, there is one final analogy we would like to share with you: It is the apt comparison between two modes of travel that we feel goes a long way toward explaining the power of the Team business over the lives we were previously living in "corporate America." The comparison is between riding a bicycle and flying a jet.

When we were taught the Industrial Age mantra of "go to school, get good grades, get a good job with benefits, keep our noses clean and retire 45 years later," we were indoctrinated into the world of *bicycle riding*. And we were recruited into this world by a bunch of other bicycle riders. It's not that we weren't making it riding our bikes; we were – kind of. We just had to pedal the bikes we were on day after day, year after year, decade after decade, drafting behind a thousand other bike-riders ahead of us in the corporate pyramid.

When we were introduced to the concepts that grew to become the Team business, we were brought into a whole new world of speed and maneuverability: flying a jet! But many of our bike riding associates said, "Look at all those crashed jets! Don't you watch the news? Those things can fall out of the air! And they're expensive! Besides, look at all the progress we're making on these bikes each day, why, when we catch a downhill now and then we can hit up to thirty miles an hour! *We're doing pretty good.*"

"Yeah," we would answer timidly, "but this is a *really long* bike ride. I mean, 45 years! We haven't even been alive that long yet! Wouldn't a jet ride be worth it?"

"Aw, I don't know," they'd say. "It takes a long time to learn how to fly a jet. I'm not sure I could find the time to take the lessons."

"But it's a long term race we're in. So what if we have to invest some time up front. Once we get to travel at five-hundred miles-an-hour we can quickly make up for lost time!"

"I'll wait and see how you do," they would say.

So we went off to take pilot's lessons. Only we didn't have to quit riding our bikes by day. We could continue riding our bikes to pay the short term expenses of living, but at night, under the cover of "dork-ness," we were practicing to become jet pilots! We don't encourage people to throw down their bikes the minute they hear about the Team business and start practicing flying full-time. It's reckless and it's unnecessary. It's a part-time training system, learned "on-the-fly" so to speak (we couldn't help that one).

Along the way, we saw a few would-be pilots that thought learning to fly was just as easy as learning to ride a bike. Because they had learned to pedal with just a little help from Mom or Dad, they figured they could learn to fly a jet much the same way. "We don't need your training system," they'd say. "We know how transportation works. Have you seen what good bike riders we are? We're just going to apply our expertise from *that*." Or they'd say, "When all my bike riding friends find out I'm doing this jet flying stuff, they'll flock to the airport to become pilots just because I'm there."

"Okay," we said confusedly. "But we're going to follow this proven training system for becoming pilots. We're not so sure we know everything yet, so we're going to listen to those with thousands of successful hours of flying under their belts."

Over time, we never saw any of those "self-taught" pilots flying the friendly skies. That's because learning to ride a bike is relatively easy. Any kid can learn it. But flying a jet must be learned from experts, from people who know how to do it. Flying a jet is not child's play. And bike riders are not capable of teaching anyone how to fly a jet.

"Are you still learning to fly a jet?" our associates would ask from time to time.

"Yep."

"Flown one yourself yet?"

"Not yet. But we're right on schedule."

"Why do you persist?" they would ask.

To which we'd reply, after a pause for effect, "Because no matter how good you get at riding a bike, you'll never *fly* on a bike."

As we began learning to fly a jet, we met others like us who joined us in our journey into the skies. What we discovered is that *inside every person destined to be an entrepreneur is the feeling that they were meant to fly.* Bikes were fine for other people, but they weren't enough for those destined to be pilots.

Once we'd learned to fly a jet, and once we experienced the exhilarating speeds and the fun of soaring upwards in life, we realized that becoming good at riding a bike is much riskier than taking to the air in a jet. That's because if you get good enough at riding a bike, you might grow accustomed to it and begin thinking it's all you were cut out to do. Soaring was for others. You were meant to play it safe on the ground, slow and steady. Besides, it's not *that* bad on the ground, is it?

But once you know you can fly, you'll never be happy riding a bike again.

A Call to Action

We wrote this book not only to teach you *how* to do something, but also to inspire *you* to do it! Learn to fly! You can do it! Let this book and the information provided within become a call to action in your life. Let it initiate a great season of learning and earning, as well as of living and giving.

Don't blow your shot.

Develop a sense of urgency.

Decide to pursue your destiny.

And never let anybody steal your dream.

Remember this: **Who dares wins**.

If you dare, we'll see you on the victory podium!

We'll see you in the skies!

Personal Story

Names: Doug and Sheri Stroh
Former Occupations: Retail Sales Business Owner;
Mortgage Loan Officer

Two men came to my home on a Wednesday night. I had no idea that the business they were going to show me would propel me out of a seventy-hour a week retail furniture store business I owned. I was consumed by debt; my wife Sheri worked full-time; we had very little time to spend together as a family, and so there was no time to enjoy our supposedly "big" six figure income. I didn't know that this business would allow us to experience an even larger income than we were used to. But much more importantly, it allowed us to buy back the time in our lives that we would have spent at our jobs.

This business and the Team system has given us the ability to pay off our debt, buy back our time, and live the life of our dreams; all while giving others the same hope and opportunity to live their lives by their *priorities* rather than their *obligations*.

Our first Major Function, along with the friendships and mentors we gained through the business, gave us the belief that the future was in our hands if we harnessed the power of a team. We thank Orrin and Laurie Woodward and Chris and Terri Brady for the work and the knowledge that they have put into our future and the future of many others. We are not just becoming great business owners, but also great leaders, parents, and spouses, living our lives by faith in God and the security of the Information Age.

Don't let the future pass you by. This is it!

"Never doubt that a small group of thoughtful, committed people can change the world. Indeed, it is the only thing that ever has."
- Margaret Mead

"You may have to fight a battle more than once to win it."
- Margaret Thatcher

"Obstacles don't have to stop you. If you run into a wall, don't turn around and give up. Figure out how to climb it, go through it, or work around it."
- Michael Jordan

"The heights by great men reached and kept were not attained by sudden flight, but they, while their companions slept, were toiling upward in the night."
- Henry Wadsworth Longfellow

"You look them straight in the eye and say, 'Don't tell me it's impossible until after I've already done it.'"
- Pam Lantos

Name: UNFOCUSED FRANK
Quote: "What?"

While the techniques and approaches suggested have worked for others, no one can guarantee that these techniques and approaches will work for you. We hope, however, that these ideas assist you in developing a strong and profitable business.